ESPRESSO
COFFEE
updated PROFESSIONAL TECHNIQUES

HOW TO IDENTIFY AND CONTROL EACH
FACTOR TO PERFECT ESPRESSO COFFEE IN A
COMMERCIAL ESPRESSO PROGRAM

DAVID C. SCHOMER

C
CLASSIC DAY
PUBLISHING

Seattle, Washington
Portland, Oregon
Denver, Colorado
Vancouver, B.C.
Scottsdale, Arizona
Minneapolis, Minnesota

ISBN: 1-59404-031-1
Library of Congress Control Number: 2004106687

Printed in the United States of America
Formerly published by Peanut Butter Publishing

For additional copies or information contact:
David C. Schomer
901 East Denny Way #100
Seattle, Washington 98122

Design: David Marty Design
Editors: Bob Brightwell and Deb Caletti

CLASSIC DAY
PUBLISHING

Classic Day Publishing
2100 Westlake Avenue North, Suite 106
Seattle, Washington 98109
800-328-4348
www.classicdaypublishing.com
Email: info@classicdaypublishing.com

TABLE OF CONTENTS

This book is dedicated
to my father James W. Schomer
who taught me scientific discipline
and a sense of wonder,
my mother Phyllis Dorrine Schomer
who gave me love and writing,
and Nancy Lee Schomer,
a gourmet cook who inspired me
to taste things.

ACKNOWLEDGMENTS

I have so many to thank I do not know where to begin, but I must start with my wife and business partner Geneva Sullivan, who is kind enough to do the work of running Espresso Vivace so I can play with coffee.

Let me thank the great baristi who present our coffee to the world, each one an artist at heart: Teal Allan, Linda Cleckler, Brian Fairbrother, Kasey Frix, Mary Gallagher, Erin Hulbert, Brian Jackson, Jodi Jaecks, Darren Johnson, Althea Jones, Don Jones, Kiley Kiebert, Robert Kyle, Christie Leigh-Kendall, Scott McDonald, Jeffrey MacIsaac, Mary Michaud, Lisa Parsons, Tricia Rhodes, Jennifer Rice, Darcy Rubel, Mary Sandstrom, Rene Sturdevant, Jodi Taylor, and Hannah Vaughan.

Let me thank my head roaster Daniel Reid for his very consistent work, and a special thanks to Corey Holt for managing the shipping department.

Thanks to you Elliott Wolf for facilitating the publishing of both editions of this book.

Over the years Kent Bakke and John Blackwell have been very supportive of my zany schemes to improve espresso coffee.

Editing: Bob Brightwell, Deb Caletti

Photography: Gregory Clark, Christopher Conrad, David Schomer

Graphics: Ron Niederkorn, dniederkor@aol.com

Design and layout: David Marty Design

PREFACE

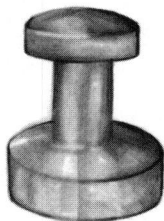

Dear Espresso Lover,

Thank you for taking a look at my updated version of ESPRESSO COFFEE: Professional Techniques.

The body of espresso technique first published in February 1996 remains useful for the majority of espresso machines in the world today. Perhaps it represents a little revolution, grinding by the cup, keeping equipment clean, and using coffee within ten days after roasting in search of a flavor and aroma sensation that comes close to the fragrant promise of the bean itself.

But now we are through the looking glass. The technological barrier built into all espresso machines to date—drifting brewing water temperature—has been breached. With the designing of the first espresso machine stable to within one degree Fahrenheit (The TREUH "Italia" designed by Mark Barnett) it becomes necessary to update the book.

Espresso Vivace has been brewing since the spring of 2001, using LaMarzocco semi-automatic espresso machines outfitted with PID controllers, (combined with my group head modification of 1995, and a pre-heat tank to avoid thermal "turbulence" in the coffee boiler), to stabilize the boiler temperature to within 3/10ths of a degree Fahrenheit. These machines produce very sweet espresso with unique characteristics. I have not published my observations on the techniques brought to the fore by the technology, simply because no one else could access machines this stable.

Well, welcome to my world. Here is all that you will need to know to make the most out of temperature-stabilized equipment.

Enjoy,
David Schomer

I
INTRODUCTION

IN THE BEGINNING, THERE WAS COFFEE ... SORT OF

My earliest memory of coffee came as a child growing up in the Wallingford district in North Seattle. I vividly remember trundling down Sunnyside Avenue, clutching my mother's hand, turning right on 45th Street and walking to the Food Giant.

Squiggling free of my mom, I dashed to the center of the store where the coffee machine, dressed in a coat of fire-engine-red paint, stood as big as a house in my four year-old eyes.

Soon my mother arrived and held a brown paper bag under the chute. Then, with a great humming sound, like a Hoover Upright, out came the fresh ground coffee, infusing the air with an aroma so rich and exotic it seemed to promise a mysterious new world—a world filled with my imagined pleasures of adulthood.

Years later my folks let me try the actual brew: coffee. Yow! It tasted like burnt matches! What did the adults do to it? This can't be right, how can anything smell so rich and taste so bad?

After this great letdown in life, I did not acquire a taste for coffee until I was a student at the University of Washington in 1980. By then the Wet Whisker had opened on Pier 70, with fresh roasted coffee beans for sale and coaching on making good drip coffee. Thus, the specialty coffee stampede had begun.

CAFFE ESPRESSO

Espresso has at least two meanings in Italian. One being fast or rapid, the second meaning, a bit archaic and perhaps from a more gentle era, is something pre-

pared especially for you, a custom creation to please you. Caffe espresso, then, is a cup of coffee prepared quickly and especially for you.

These shades of meaning were relayed to me on the train heading into Rome by Italian food critic Bruno Moschella, who spoke with great enthusiasm punctuated by quick stabbing gestures of his reading glasses.

The year was 1989 and I was on my first of two trips to Italy to study caffe espresso traditions and practice. To be sure, the Italians were not amused by my antics in their Gran Bars—taking pictures, knocking over the sugar bowls and asking far too many questions about caffe espresso.

Ridiculous! It's just coffee, was the unspoken attitude of the stylish baristas I was pestering. But after tasting, and documenting, espresso coffee in hundreds of bars from Naples to Trieste, I felt like I was getting to know what the various Italian espresso styles were supposed to taste like.

After returning to Seattle I began to refine what I had learned in Italy by practicing at my own espresso bars. With espresso coffee, I found that the more I learned the less I knew.

My discovery is that the creation of caffe espresso is a very delicate and exacting culinary art which is widely misunderstood outside of Italy. And ... the Italians aren't talking. Properly used, the espresso machine and burr grinder represent the ultimate culmination of humanity's four-century exploration of methods to capture the aromatic essence of roasted coffee in a cup.

One reason for the lack of standard practice in making caffe espresso is that it is so new. The potential of the coffee rivals that of wine in its sophistication and complexity, but wine traditions and practice are thousands of years old.

By comparison, espresso tradition is a culinary infant. I date the arrival of caffe espresso on the world stage to 1947, when the Gaggia company of Italy achieved pressurized brewing water with a spring piston. Italian machines for coffee had been using steam pressure since the early Bezzara and Pavoni designs were debuted in Milano in 1906. Direct steam pressure meant the brewing water was too hot, destroying most of the coffee oils in an effort to produce the coffee. And on occasion, the machines exploded.

For purposes of clarity, I call the coffee from this era *caffe expres,* because it was made one cup at a time, expressly for the customer. But the cream coffee, true

espresso, did not arrive until brewing pressure and temperature were made independently variable in 1947.

Caffe espresso has the potential to be the pinnacle of all coffee making methods because of its unique ability to extract the maximum flavor from coffee and leave behind bitter compounds and caffeine. It is the pressure that does it. But there is absolutely no standard practice outside of Italy. All over the world people are buying these fancy machines with no concept of their true potential. With great care, *espresso can be made to taste exactly like ground coffee smells,* only more so. A honey-thick nectar at best, combining the experiences of flavor and texture. But its pursuit is a very fickle affair.

It has been sung by many a bard that you can search the world over to try to find true love, the pure emotion of exquisite rarity indeed. Well, let me just add to that short list. You can search the world over for good espresso, and you may grow old before finding a great cup. This book is an effort to correct the situation.

A Culinary Revolution

Before we get into the details of making the rarefied nectar, let's take a brief look at the cultural context in which the people of the States currently find themselves.

We are in the midst of a quiet cultural renaissance. People across the U.S., and particularly in the Northwest, have had enough of canned, preground coffee, beers that have all the body of lemonade, and bread that is fluorescent white, flavorless, and tears nicely down the middle.

Despite the magic of Madison Avenue image-making, people are moving away from industrial, pre-packaged foods. Fresh-baked bread, micro-breweries and small local coffee roasters are some of the trends right now in the culinary culture of the U.S. People want true freshness and are willing to pay for it.

This little renaissance is rooted in some very Old World ideas where small is beautiful and freshness dominates the quality of what we eat and drink. It is the perfect form for a small business as well, our passion and care pitted against big marketing-driven companies and their perfectly deceptive image-making. With each new micro-roaster that pops up, there exists another soldier in the war against culinary poverty.

So, hurrah for fresh cuisines. But in espresso making there is a danger.

Nothing is as bad as bad espresso. Being so concentrated, mistakes result is concentrated bitterness. Without respect for the coffee and a passionate attention to detail, espresso could be just another passing fad, a flash in the pan in the developing history of culture.

WHO THE HECK IS THIS CHEEKY FELLOW, ANYWAY?

To help you properly use the information in this book, I should let you know some of my own biases and quirks and tell you a little about my background. After all, if you have yet to taste my coffee, why should you trust what I have to say about espresso preparation?

Although I was raised in and around Seattle, I still like to call myself a Kent boy, after the rural area located just to the south of the Emerald City where I lived during my formative high school days. A Kent boy, by definition, is a creature given to courtesy and punctuality and one who you can rely on to feed the chickens in sub-zero weather.

By 1982, I had amassed some background and training in *metrology*—literally, the science of measurement. Over a span of eight years, I worked primarily with electrical parameters of DC resistance, current and voltage. This work was performed in the United States Air Force, John Fluke Manufacturing in Everett, Washington, and at Boeing's Class A Standards Lab in Seattle.

Equipment that I was calibrating and repairing was capable of accurate resolutions finer than one part per million. So taken was I by the very essence of precision, I wrote a poem entitled "Light Beam Galvanometer," which you will be mercifully spared from reading today.

In a brave effort to forestall further burdens of adulthood, I also dedicated twelve years of my life to an intensive study of classical flute performance. This passion led to a degree in music and several recording projects with a classical guitarist. It was a fine extension of childhood for me, but as a flutist I suffered from a late start and a lack of talent. Not even my Kent boy work ethic could overcome these twin realities.

When I started a coffee company in April of 1988, my approach to espresso was formed from these two disciplines which can be summed up in a tidy little sound bite: *scientific precision guided by artistry.* Caffe espresso is scientific in the

sense of compiling a body of technique based on trial and error, but science cannot tell you how the coffee should taste.

My research on how to make a perfect espresso includes two trips to Northern Italy, as well as hounding anyone in my hometown who knew anything on the subject. Then, at my own espresso bars in Seattle, I estimate that I have prepared over 350,000 espresso coffees in the past fifteen years, usually under critical conditions. And, this is ongoing.

My fascination with a perfect espresso never ends. Current research fronts include measuring and stabilizing the brewing water temperature as it permeates the coffee itself, as well as my ongoing efforts to find the perfect grinder.

For myself, the espresso making and presentation are an art not unlike music. In a perfect espresso ristretto, qualities of flavor and texture seem to merge. The most delicate of the aromatic flavors are captured in the crema for just a moment, savored at once, and then remembered in the sweet lingering aftertaste.

My Espresso Style

First and always foremost: All information is geared to making an espresso that is characterized by a heavy red-brown syrup called crema. This crema features an intense coffee flavor that is free of bitterness. Ideally, *espresso should taste like the freshly ground coffee smells.* Texture is featured always, and should feel like a pair of velvet pajamas wrapped around your tongue.

I am partial to Northern Italian coffee roasting and blending traditions. In this style, the beans are roasted to a deep mahogany brown, but no coffee oils are present on the surface of the freshly roasted beans. This style develops the most caramelized sugars within the beans then quickly halts the roast before the nutty bite of roasting overwhelms the natural sweetness. Beans must be carefully selected to be low in acidity for this style to be a success.

The goal in blending is a balanced, complex flavor in which the negative aspects of some coffee beans are countered and complemented by other beans in the mix. A sweet, complex flavor with a mellow aftertaste is the hallmark of a fine blend. The coffee flavor should be balanced so that no single element dominates the cup.

This is an important distinction to make. Darker roasts, a deep brown with a

light sheen of oil on the surface such as found in southern Italy and as far north as Naples, offer more "roasting flavor" in the final cup.

Espresso made from very dark roasted coffee, such as what is called French Roast in the United States where the beans are oily-looking and almost black, features a smoky bite in the finished cup of coffee. In this style, the roasting bite dominates the more subtle and sweet varietal differences in the coffee. Roasts such as these are intensely bitter as caffe espresso. Put in a large mug of steamed milk and you have something close to French Cafe Au Lait.

The ideal in the Northern Italian tradition is when roasting bite and varietal flavors are perfectly balanced in the final cup.

Unlike the traditions of fine wine, art has to happen twice to achieve a fine cup of espresso. At the vineyard, wine is created and bottled by a master wine maker, an artist taking pride in a fine creation. When the bottle is opened and served, if it has been properly stored, the wine should be close to its potential.

When coffee is roasted, blended and packaged, it is completely at the mercy of the person preparing it. In my experience, it is more difficult to make good espresso consistently than it is to roast the coffee. Likewise, you, the barista, are totally dependent on the quality standards of the roaster and blender of your coffee. A world class espresso blend can be very easily destroyed by an untrained barista, and the best coffee maker cannot rise above the coffee being used to make the shot.

FACTORS IN A PERFECT CUP

My approach to lead you into the world of espresso is to break down the process into identifiable factors that affect quality. Bear in mind that this is an abstraction necessary to organize a lot of information. It does not mean that these factors are all-encompassing or totally defined.

For example, pump pressure is composed of many sub factors that for the purpose of discussion, we just assume are OK. It implies that the valves in the machine seal perfectly and that your gaskets are all soft and pliable, providing a good seal. We are assuming a working pump, and on and on. In REALITY everything tends to squirm around on you from time to time. So try not to let your mind fixate on the abstract categories that we must use to break down the prob-

lem. Learn the basic playing field by reading the book through and reconstruct the elements to form an espresso program.

The reality of espresso making is that it is very hard to isolate factors when other factors are all out of whack. The factors all interrelate and affect each other. To paraphrase Dr. Ernesto Illy, it is an equation with over a million possibilities for error, and only one combination results in a perfect solution.

As a practical matter, read the book through. Try to understand the information given in the context in which it truly exists, as a mess of factors or variables that profoundly affect each other and complicate the equation by squirming around on you from time to time.

To achieve a good espresso, it is essential not to dwell on a single factor. To be successful, you must remain aware of all the factors and how they interrelate. As Musashi, the great Japanese strategist has said, "Do not fix the eyes."

Here is the working list of factors that affect your espresso coffee. I will use these factors to organize the information in this book:

A. Environmental factors
    1. Humidity
    2. Temperature
    3. Direct sunlight

B. Equipment factors
    4. Grinder burrs
    5. Pump pressure
    6. Water temperature
    7. Machine cleanliness

C. Ingredient factors
    8. Water purity/mineral content
    9. Coffee freshness
    10. Roasting degree
    11. Blend

D. Barista techniques
    12. Packing the coffee
    13. Dosage of coffee
    14. Elapsed time for the shot
    15. Shot cutoff point
    16. Adjusting the grind
    17. Cleaning techniques

So get nice and comfortable, curl up with a cup of tea, and come with me into my world where we will learn how to make a tiny, honey-thick cup of coffee that tastes just like fresh roasted coffee smells ... only more so.

II
Espresso Theory
Establishing a Framework for Knowledge

What's a course without a little theory? It's a jumble of facts with no cohesive framework, I would say.

In teaching people to make espresso, I have learned that their ability to reproduce quality coffee on their own in their own shops increases greatly if I began each training session with a basic theoretical framework. This kind of background provides them with a broad understanding of the many problems they will face in making great espresso.

Why is Making Espresso So Tricky?

Most problems you will encounter in your journey toward espresso excellence will be related to two unavoidable facts: water is lazy and coffee flavor compounds are volatile.

The Hydraulic Problem: Lazy Water

Espresso is tricky because you are dealing with pressurized water coming into contact with a thin wafer of ground coffee. A modern espresso machine applies water at 120 to 130 pounds of force to a cake of packed coffee less than 1/2 inch thick.

Much of the technique presented in this book has to do with *creating an even resistance to pressurized water,* which, as a result of its lazy nature, will try to find a way to sneak through the ground coffee and avoid the work of extracting your

soluble coffee oils. The slightest irregularity in the density of the coffee or the tiniest pit in the top of the cake will give your pressurized water an avenue of escape.

Water, by nature seeks the path of least resistance.

In the mild case, some sections of the packed coffee are over-extracted, contributing bitter compounds after the flavor has been exhausted. At the same time, denser areas in the coffee will not contribute their flavor oils to the cup. In this scenario, the espresso pour may feature white streaks and have higher surface tension. The crema becomes thin and does not hang straight down from the spouts. The heavy flow of perfect espresso will turn into a corkscrew pattern. It clings briefly to the tip, due to higher surface tension, and literally sucks in towards the edge of the spout a bit. In addition, espresso so afflicted may feature whitish streaks in with the rich red brown crema, and shorter shot volumes.

In the extreme case, slightly brown water comes gushing out like a toilet overflowing, and the corresponding flavor of the coffee fits the simile perfectly. This is caused by the coffee not presenting an even resistance to the water or the grind being way too coarse.

A Diagram For Success

Take a look at the accompanying diagram for a schematic understanding of what's going on.

Imagine in diagram 1 that you are looking at a cross section of a double group basket loaded with a pile of fresh ground coffee from the grinder.

In diagram 2, you see that the coffee has been carefully leveled off and distributed to feature an *even density before packing.* This critical step I call "loose coffee distribution." (Even very experienced baristas often mess this up by rushing too quickly and jarring the loose coffee before packing. More on this in *Chapter XII: Espresso Packing* and *Chapter XIII: Espresso Dosing.)*

In diagram 3, you see the coffee packed to a very even underlying density indicated by the shaded graphics. The coffee has been hard-packed with a good twist of the packer and dosed correctly so a little gap exists between its surface and the bottom of the dispersion screen where the water comes out.

Then the pump is activated.

IDEALIZED EXTRACTION SERIES

1 LOOSE GROUND
COFFEE.

2 EVENLY DISTRIBUTED
AND DOSED.

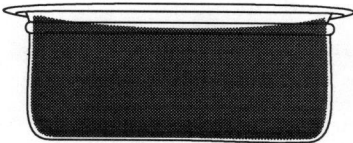

3 HARD PACKED
& POLISHED.

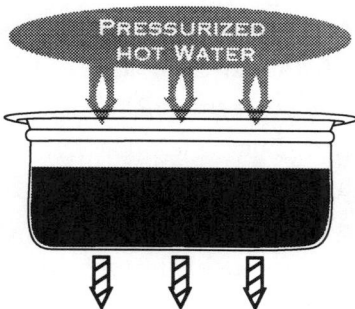

PRESSURIZED
HOT WATER

PERFECT EVEN
EXTRACTION.

At first, hot water dribbles onto the surface in the pre-infusion stage of the event. Pre-infusion is a period lasting about one second in which the hot water seeps onto the surface of the coffee before the pump "kicks in" and full pressure arrives. The Italian engineers recognized pre-infusion as necessary to help seal the top of the coffee for the blast of pressurized water to follow. Preinfusion also loosens up flavor compounds for the brewing process, enabling them to be transported into your cup.

After the initial one second goes by, a hydraulic fist smashes your coffee in the face. At 200 degrees Fahrenheit and 120 pounds of force, the water can blast coffee out of its way to create a pit, or path of lesser resistance. This can result in a watery brown gusher coming out below, or, at the very least, will result in leaving behind enough flavor to rob you of the optimum cup. Over-extracted sections in the packed coffee will quickly exhaust their booty of flavor, and begin to ooze bitter flavor into the cup.

Remember that our theoretical diagram is an ideal. In the real world, many different factors can drastically affect resistance to water, including packing, dosing, coffee freshness, grind setting, grinder burrs and humidity.

Controlling all of these factors, and understanding how they interrelate, is the only way to assure that the brewing water meets hard-packed coffee which offers an even resistance. Then for the next 25 seconds or so, the pressurized water oozes through the coffee and out comes perfect espresso into the cup.

Coffee Flavor Volatility

The rich smell of fresh-ground coffee has been the inspiration of the bards for centuries. The difficulty of capturing this aromatic essence in a cup has also inspired an avalanche of beautiful and bizarre coffee making devices.

Why is a cup of coffee so difficult to make as rich as it smells? It is the volatility of the aromatic oils that constitute coffee flavor. These rich, earthy-smelling compounds that envelop your senses when you stick your nose in the freshly ground coffee are very unstable and easy to offend.

Brief exposure to air will cause flavors to become rancid through oxidation. Too high a brewing temperature will burn these compounds, and too low a temperature will cause coffee flavors to be sour to the taste, for just a few examples.

So the biggest problem has always been to make coffee without destroying the coffee oils.

In coffee making of any type, freshness of the bean is the dominant factor in producing a perfect cup. In espresso, this is most apparent. Espresso machines offer a very concentrated coffee liqueur. If the oils are destroyed and turn bitter, this bitterness will be highly concentrated by your espresso machine. Roasted coffee itself contains compounds that will destroy the delicate flavors. In espresso, the game is to *separate with the greatest efficiency the flavor oils from destructive compounds present in ground coffee.*

ESPRESSO AS ART

This is where espresso becomes art—understanding coffee flavors and seducing them into a cup. Too complex to classify and too numerous to list, coffee flavors are a chimera to the plodding science of chemistry. They must be understood intuitively and cherished to be conjured into your cup.

Factors affecting the survival of the aromatic flavors are:

1. Brewing water temperature.
2. Rate of extraction (brewing time).
3. Volume of the shot (cutoff point).
4. Coffee freshness.
5. Machine cleanliness.
6. Roasting degree.

It is important to understand that none of these factors stand alone. They are all affected by each other. Changes in one can result in changes in the others. When you are going through these factors one by one, always keep in mind the two key facts: water is lazy and coffee flavor is volatile.

A CALL TO ENGINEERS

Over the years at Espresso Vivace, as we have improved our ability to control the factors influencing our coffee, brewing water temperature has emerged as the single factor needing the most improvement from the manufacturers of espresso machines.

Sometimes, if you get amazing shots of espresso, (we refer to as "God Coffee") espresso coffee that tastes so rich and earthy, so much like it smells, that a fellow might drop the cup and burst out laughing, but more often you do not, it is brewing water temperature drifting around on you. This inconsistency is built into most of the machines sold in the world today.

It is my contention that the coffee is very sensitive to changes in brewing water temperature during the brew cycle as small as 1 degree Fahrenheit. However, most of the machines feature stability of temperature no better than 8 degrees during a shot.* This is clearly not good enough.

In regards to temperature stability, espresso machines featuring a dedicated boiler are superior to all heat exchange machines tested to date.

In *Chapter VII: Brewing Water Temperature,* we will examine techniques to coax better temperature stability from the espresso machine.

How Do I Use This Book?

I approach the complex art of espresso by identifying the factors that affect the brewing process, and trying to control those factors for best results. I have also made a personal religion of espresso's interrelated complexity. Stated simply, you cannot isolate a factor until all the other factors are in your control. This fact raises the question: where do I start to improve my espresso?

Just one example of the factors hiding within one another is that espresso made using stale coffee beans will look exactly like fresh coffee made with dull grinder burrs. Each produces whitish-looking crema featuring higher surface tension, compared to the beautiful red-brown nectar of a well-made espresso.

I do not mean to imply that making espresso coffee is a science. It is, rather, a culinary art. I say this after fifteen years of daily, total immersion in high-vol-

---

*As of this revision, February 2004, a machine capable of temperature stability better than 1 degree F. has been built in Seattle. The TREUH Company, and engineer Mark Barnett, have created a near perfect brewing system using small dedicated boilers, stabilized by PID controllers, for each group head. Thank you, thank you dear sweet engineer. All measurements are made on the coffee bed using a Fluke K/J Digital Thermometer fitted with a K-type thermocouple bead probe.

ume espresso work. To capture the volatile aromatics present in ground coffee you must tease and cajole them into our cup. You must understand the coffee intuitively. From the moment a coffee bean is roasted, then ground and brewed, it is undergoing continuous chemical transformation. The finest and most noble flavors are very delicate, fleeting compounds. Pure science depends on defining and then quantifying compounds for analysis. How can you define or analyze something that is in continuous change? My answer is you cannot.

Caffe espresso must be cherished and pursued tirelessly to be seduced into a cup.

With so many interrelated factors affecting your coffee it can be bewildering to implement improvements. Like Houdini facing a series of locks, sequencing your approach is critical.

SEQUENCING IMPROVEMENTS

Here is the sequence we followed at our operation, starting in 1988:

First we learned to hand pack the coffee. We ground each order for the customer, learned to dose and distribute the coffee evenly by volume. And we started with good water filtration. (I am still working on a ground coffee doser that will not expose the coffee to air.)

After working the packing, grinding and dosing into a training program, we started looking at extraction rate and extraction volume. Here we arrived at the conclusion that we needed to serve only double shots. We mastered the slow and short pour, and like most Americans we were surprised at how diminutive a well-made espresso is. So, we served double coffee in all espresso coffees we prepared. We were pouring less than two ounces of crema in 25 to 30 seconds using about 17 grams of hand-packed, freshly ground coffee.

It quickly became clear that keeping the machine clean was essential. We began our schedule of cleaning every four hours, and soaking the porta-filters each night in a solution of espresso detergent and water. During this phase, we also learned to remove dispersion screens and clean the group heads beneath them each evening. (In 1992 I figured out how to rinse the group head after each shot to release stored coffee oils trapped by brewing, and to scrub the porta-filter every 40 minutes.)

From a trip to Italy I learned that grinder burrs will become dull and must be

replaced periodically. We set up a schedule to replace our parallel burrs every 500 pounds of coffee we ground on them. Conical burrs will last up to 2,000 pounds before becoming dull.

With new grinder burrs in place, it became obvious that we saw a great decrease in crema if the coffee got warm during storage or was used more than ten days after roasting. We convinced our roaster to deliver twice weekly and write the roasting date on each bag we bought. (Vivace did not begin roasting until 1991.)

After controlling freshness and grinder burrs, I noticed a lemony brightness in the espresso, particularly compared to the Northern Italian coffee I had recently tasted in Milano. I asked my roaster what it was and he said it was acidity. He began making a Vivace blend with very low acidity, and roasted to the mahogany-brown color, which I had seen in Milano and Trieste.

By 1990 I began to focus on sourness in some shots we prepared. The color of these sour shots was also different, a cinnamon-brown rather than a red-brown. Because the problem was intermittent, I suspected brewing water temperature was the culprit. I created an espresso coffee thermometer by placing a tiny bead probe into the surface of the packed coffee and monitoring brewing temperature as we worked the bar. I found out that coffee roasted to Northern Italian color was sour when brewed between 199 and 202 degrees Fahrenheit. Below 199 it was simply flat. The ideal brewing temperature is 203.5 degrees Fahrenheit.

My thermometer and I have raised quite a fuss since then. It turns out that all espresso machines have widely varying temperatures of brewing water as it permeates the coffee. The worst machine I have tested, a very popular Italian heat-exchange design, displayed temperatures from 177 to 213 degrees Fahrenheit, over a 20-minute period of making continuous shots. All the machines feature more stable brewing water temperatures when making shots one right after another.

During 1995, using my own innovations, my LaMarzocco semi-automatic machines were improved to a temperature accuracy of +/- 1.5 degrees Fahrenheit, (a three degree range of error) regardless of volume served. In 2001 we applied PID controllers to our modified LaMarzocco design, and attached a pre-heat tank for the water entering the coffee boiler. These prototypes are very stable, with the

total variation within one degree of error. These machines are capable of producing sweet espresso every shot, but it remains far from easy to do so.

Now, finally, espresso professionals have a machine available that will meet or exceed this incredible performance—the TREUH "Italia," designed by Mark Barnett. This is the first truly stable machine, and I expect a lot more to enter the market in the next ten years. Automatic steamers are great, but how about actually helping the espresso taste good?

In 1991 I began experimenting with conical burr grinders. I noticed a strange phenomenon as my attention was directed to the grinder doser. At my busy bar, we were grinding more than 30 pounds a day and the coffee would invariably become thin once exposed to air for an hour. It was great, thick and delicious when we opened. But after just one hour of production it became thin and whitish. The conical burr grinders helped, but did not eliminate the problem. I traced the problem to excess motor heat. The grinder motor was heating up the burrs and we were losing quality and value as coffee oils were degraded during grinding.

I located a belt-driven grinder to eliminate motor heat from being conducted up the metal drive shaft into the burrs. To handle convected heat, I fitted each grinder with a computer-type silent running vent fan that draws heated air out of the case of the grinder.

In 1993 we noticed that if anyone flushed the toilet, our brewing pressure would drop. We fixed that with "static-tanks," Water tanks, made of stainless steel and holding 2.5 gallons each, that would automatically re-fill when drawn down a bit.

This, with some jumping about a bit on my chronology, is the actual sequence of improvements we made. After temperature was stabilized, serious work on the blends could commence because I could finally taste caffe espresso with the precision of the cupping method.

Espresso improvements hide within one another, like Ukrainian nested dolls. A program with a gross error, like stale coffee, or dirty machines, is dominated by that factor until it is fixed. You cannot see the difference a better packing tool makes, for example, if your program is dominated by a major factor which is out of your control.

So I ask you for your trust in the beginning of your improvements. Start with packing techniques, replace grinder burrs, and go through the factors on faith. As your program nears perfection you will see the results more clearly in the cup, until you arrive at temperature control, which is largely built into the machine you are using. At that point if you are happy, we have succeeded. If not, you will need to replace the machine.

ENVIRONMENTAL FACTORS

III
ENVIRONMENTAL FACTORS
AIR TEMPERATURE, SUNLIGHT AND HUMIDITY

WHAT IS A FACTOR?

A factor in espresso making is any element that affects the quality of espresso in the cup and which must be accounted for throughout the entire espresso making process. Some of these factors are variables, often environmental in nature, which can change from moment to moment. The variable nature of these factors requires corresponding adjustments by the barista in order to maintain quality. Other factors are techniques which are performed, with varying degrees of success, by the human hand.

THE NOT-SO-GREAT OUTDOORS

I started my business in 1988 as an outdoor cart, and I quickly discovered that the effects of the environment are much more drastic when working outdoors with espresso than they are when working indoors. Our research shows that periods of cool weather and medium humidity (around 50 to 60 percent) are quite forgiving for coffee making. Coffee ground in these conditions can retain its full aroma and character for up to four minutes after grinding.

It is important to remember, however, that coffee is finicky and so is the weather. Oxidation begins instantly as you grind and dose your coffee.

During hot weather, for example, coffee goes stale more quickly. This is especially true of ground coffee. The worst conditions for espresso making are when you have high temperatures, sun shining on the beans and dry air. Under these

conditions, water molecules evaporate from the coffee as you grind it at such a high rate that they seem to strip away volatile flavor compounds, robbing your coffee of a great deal of the flavor.

Compensating for these conditions is a bit of a compromise, at best. It comes down to precision. Be careful to grind just the right amount for the shot, leaving no ground coffee sitting in the dosing hopper for the next order. Keep the top on the dosing hopper, even sealing it with a bit of duct tape. Be quick in dosing and packing the coffee, giving the dry air minimum time to affect the ground coffee. At Espresso Vivace, we have discovered that the only way to get the best of the bean is to grind the coffee per order. Yes, this means by the cup.

Even with all these precautions, while working outdoors in late August, we have a difficult time producing the perfect hanging pours of October. Gourmet espresso is really more of an indoor sport where you have some control over your environment. The espresso cart phenomenon, in my opinion, is probably a passing fad for this reason.

The effects of high temperatures and low humidity are equally devastating to whole bean coffee.

Under these conditions, order coffee from your roaster more often, maybe every five days or so. Keep your stock of beans sealed and in a cellar or some other relatively cool, dark place. (We will examine coffee storage in detail in our discussion of coffee freshness.)

In late August on the carts in Seattle, we would put into the hopper about two cups of whole bean coffee at a time, enough so that we would use it up every fifteen minutes or so. If the sun was shining on the bean hoppers, we would line the hopper above the grinder with a sheet of white paper. Be aware that your coffee suffers from heat and sunlight. Baby it a bit.

Baby, It's Cold Outside

Another big challenge was making the espresso sweet in colder weather. When it's cold outside, the porta-filters tend to be much colder than they would be at room temperature indoors. On all espresso machines the spouts and body of the group handle and porta-filter are exposed to the environment, and the metal radiates heat. Although all machines are designed to keep this important

"brewing basket" warm, winter weather will tend to cool it down more than ten degrees, even when in the machine.

In espresso making, the ideal situation would be to have the temperature a consistent value from group head all the way into the cup.

Techniques for dealing with cooler ambient temperatures surrounding the group head and handles are based on common sense:

1. Keep the group handle in the head, where it is warm, as long as possible during the coffee making process. In other words, do not use it as a conversational prop, waving it around as you yammer on with a customer. Be quick. Grind the coffee, bang out the old grounds and pack it quickly, but precisely, before it has much of a chance to cool down.

2. Preheat the group handles and heads. As you grind a shot of coffee, activate the pump and force hot water through the handle and old packed grounds. No more than two ounces of water should be used for preheating, however. Greater discharges can, and will, upset the thermal equilibrium of the espresso machine and cause a cooling of the source water.

IT'S NOT THE HEAT, IT'S THE HUMIDITY

Humidity intimately affects your operation on a moment-to-moment basis, because ground coffee is very *hygroscopic*, meaning it exchanges water molecules freely from its surrounding environment. As you grind coffee, it absorbs water molecules or gives them up to the atmosphere, depending on relative humidity surrounding the grinders. In very humid conditions, the espresso packs tighter, like matted dog hair, producing a slower extraction rate.

In espresso, we are very concerned with how much water passes per second through the ground, packed coffee. There is a golden rate of water flow, corresponding to about a 25-second extraction for a total shot, single or double, that maximizes flavor release and minimizes the amount of bitter flavors and excessive caffeine that get into the final cup. (A single or double shot will feature the same overall ideal extraction time, providing the packed coffee is the same thickness and shape in each basket.)

In our method, the coarseness of the grind is the only adjustment our baristas make to keep the extraction rate ideal. The dosage and packing weight are kept consistent to reduce variables.

The coffee is actually quite sensitive to changes in humidity. We train baristas to constantly "tune" for the optimum rate of extraction—often changing the grind slightly with each shot as maritime air sweeps off Puget Sound.

LIKE A FINELY TUNED VIOLIN

In espresso making, keep the packing weight and dosage of coffee consistent. The only thing to change in order to maintain a perfect hanging pour is the fineness of the grind.

When *humidity increases,* the coffee absorbs water and packs down tighter, which increases its resistance to the pressurized water trying to pass through. You compensate for this by making the *grind a little more coarse.*

If *humidity decreases* while you are making coffee, you need *a slightly finer grind* to maintain your creamy 25-second extraction rate.

Of course, we do not consult a gauge of relative humidity to make espresso. It is just important to know why the coffee will change its extraction rate on you during the day.

When adjusting your grind, think of yourself as a musician tuning your violin as its delicately balanced wood frame changes ever so slightly in response to increases and decreases in temperature and humidity.

EQUIPMENT FACTORS

R. Nezvigora 3/4

IV
THE ESPRESSO GRINDER

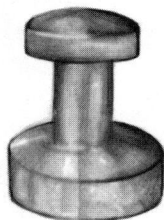

When things are not going well in espresso making, it is often difficult to identify a clear cause for the problem. The reason for this is that we are dealing with a multi-variable system in which each factor must be controlled to achieve excellence. If any one of the factors is out of whack—from stale coffee to incorrect water temperature—the espresso can be ruined.

Given this qualifier, it must be noted that the grinder is the most critical component to perfection in the cup.

WHY IS THE GRINDER SO CRITICAL?

The answer lies in the basic facts of espresso extraction: short brewing times combined with water under pressure.

BREWING TIME

For our purposes, brewing time refers to the duration of time in which hot water is allowed to permeate the ground coffee.

Ideally, in espresso making, hot pressurized water comes into contact with your ground coffee for 25 to 28 seconds. This means that your soluble aromatic coffee flavor oils have no time to slowly soak out from the ground coffee as they do in a drip pot or French Press, which have brewing times of three to five minutes.

For the coffee methods that use longer brewing times, an inexpensive blade grinder will do just fine. However, with the short, intense exposure of the espresso process, the precision of the grinder becomes much more critical. There is a much smaller margin of error, and the grinder must provide a uniform flaking of

the coffee bean. Think of it as a shearing process, where the greatest concentration of coffee oils are made available to the action of hot water because the grinder has provided the maximum surface area on a micro level. It is this convoluted, intricate surface area that enables oils to be evenly available to infuse the final cup with the greatest flavor.

WATER UNDER PRESSURE

The modem rotary pump espresso machine delivers water to the coffee at about 125 pounds of pressure, or nine atmospheres. All of this pressure comes to bear on a small cake of packed coffee less than one half inch thick. That is a lot of pressure on a small wafer of packed, ground coffee. So the other critical job of the grinder is to prepare the coffee in such a manner as to offer *even resistance* to the water.

As I have stated earlier in the book, water is lazy and will seek the path of least resistance. It wants to go down into the nice cozy drain without a care for your grand scheme of making perfect espresso. The proper grind will force the water to do its work.

To understand the complexity of this process, it is useful to look at the microphotographs of ground coffee. (Many thanks to Dan Hallett of Swedish Hospital in Seattle, Washington.)

In Photograph 1, we see coffee ground with a commercial burr grinder fitted with nice sharp burrs. You can see the complex lattice of coffee particles compared with the same grinder fitted with dull burrs, as shown in Photograph 2. A complex lattice network offers the greatest surface area for coffee oils to be exposed to the hot water.

The coffee has been sheared into shapes that maximize the surface area of the exposed coffee oils. Thus, a 25-second infusion at high pressure has the greatest opportunity to carry flavor oils to your cup before the coffee has a chance to release destructive compounds and caffeine that can make the cup bitter. The very efficiency of the espresso system is its beauty, and its beast.

Dull burrs, as shown in Photograph 2, produce irregular lumps of coffee. In a short percolation time, the hot water will wash around the big lumps and oversaturate the smaller particles. (Coffee ground on a blade grinder also produces

Photograph 1. Sharp grinder burrs maximize surface area of ground coffee.

Photograph 2. Dull burrs produce irregular lumps.

irregular sized lumps.) You will never get that perfect, oozing pour that is an index of full flavor in the cup. On a micro-level, the flavor locked in the big lumps will not be released, and the smaller particles will over saturate releasing bitter compounds into the coffee.

THE IDEAL ESPRESSO GRINDER

In case anyone ever builds one (perhaps you?), here is what I think the perfect espresso grinder needs to feature:

1. Grinding head should be composed of conical burrs for the task of reducing whole beans to small chunks, followed by flat burrs for the fine work. This is known as a mixed burr system.

2. Grinding head should be belt driven to avoid conducting heat directly from the motor up the drive shaft to the burrs. This arrangement also reduces the speed at which the burrs rotate. Rotation speed should be no more than 900RPM, and, I speculate, no less than 200RPM.

3. Motor should draw no more than 5 amps, and be engineered to turned on and off frequently without building up excessive heat.

4. Motor housing should be outfitted with a small fan to draw warm air out of the housing.

5. Dosing mechanism should be made durable for high volume use. The doser needs to feature some kind of design to help break up clumps which naturally form when grinding fresh coffee roasted to a Northern Italian degree. Doser ideally would isolate ground coffee from the air.

6. A built-in timer, which, when activated by the barista, would allow the grinder to grind just the right amount of coffee, then shut off. The timer must operate between 5 and 25 seconds and be easily adjustable with one-second intervals.

Many grinders feature an incremental adjustment mechanism in which the adjustment collar is held in place with a pin or indentation. As the burrs on these grinders begin to wear, the gaps between adjustment positions become too large. Literally, the smallest adjustment possible on such a machine may alter the extraction time by 5 to 10 seconds. A skilled barista adjusts for much finer time intervals to maintain maximum flavor and texture in the espresso (see *Chapter 16: Adjusting the Grind*).

Parallel or "flat" burrs.

Conical grinder burrs.

Combination of conical and parallel burrs is the best system we have discovered.

Combination burrs—close up.

There are two types of grinder burrs (please see photographs on page 31):

1. Flat or parallel burrs.
2. Conical burrs.

Conical burrs are thought to be superior due to their longer cutting edge which allows for a slower motor speed, thus minimizing damage from the heat of grinding. Whatever the theory, I can tell you from personal experience that conical burrs are better. When using conical burr grinders, my espresso is heavier, thicker and sweeter, and the shots are a higher volume. The machine literally delivers more flavor into my cup.

Commercial grinders feature large powerful motors that grind coffee slowly without heating up. They also feature very precise machining to assure parallel burrs and fine adjustment capability. All of this technology accounts for the high cost of commercial espresso grinders.

Maintaining Your Edge

I've been known to nag my clients about replacing dull burrs, but I nag for very good reasons. Grinder burrs have a limited useful life span. In general, the parallel burrs are toast after about 600 pounds of coffee have been ground. Conical burrs, on the other hand, may provide a good pour with up to 2000 pounds on them.

On a flat burr grinder, replace the burrs every 600 pounds of ground coffee. They cost a bit, but your coffee will love you and so will your customers.

Symptoms of dull burrs are a thin texture in the espresso and shorter shots. But remember, before you can isolate a problem to a specific cause, such as dull burrs, all the other factors in the process must be under control. For example, espresso made from stale coffee looks exactly like fresh coffee made with dull burrs.

When changing burrs, make sure that you clean the surface that the burr sits on, then evenly and gradually tighten the screws that hold the burrs in place. Do not oil the adjustment threads—this will attract crud. Merely clean the threads of all coffee particles with a scribe or pointed awl. A small wire brush may also be useful for cleaning threads.

Limitations Of The Vivace Method

The dosing mechanism on Italian espresso grinders is a cylinder designed to hold up to 200 grams of ground coffee at a time. It is designed to measure off a single or double dose by the actions of rotating fins that are driven by a ratcheting handle assembly. One click of the ratchet marks a single dose, two clicks marks a double.

This design has one major drawback: To maintain a regular density for the fins to slice off the same dose each time, the doser needs to be at least half full of ground coffee. By keeping the doser half full, however, coffee freshness is jeopardized. Remember, coffee flavors are very volatile and more than a little cranky. Pre-grinding coffee, even for a few moments, exposes the coffee oils to the air, which immediately, through the process of oxidation, begins to destroy flavor compounds.

To avoid this problem at Espresso Vivace, we grind by the cup. Then we flap the dosing lever five or six times to get all the ground coffee out. The dosers wear out quite quickly and the fins mix the coffee with air, which is not good for the coffee. Some kind of enclosed dosing chute would be ideal.

Grinding by the cup puts a strain on the motors as well, which in turn affects the coffee because all the stopping and starting creates heat. We are using the grinders in ways they are not meant to be used in a high volume commercial environment. When motors are frequently activated from a stop, extra heat is created from the capacitive discharge circuits designed to kick the motor into life. In addition, we are very hard on switches and doser components.

The heat builds up throughout the day. By mid-morning, after about ten or fifteen pounds of coffee have been ground and served, we have heat problems. The ground coffee is warm to the touch as it comes out of the burrs and into the dosing hopper. We find that the heat is destroying significant amounts of coffee flavors during the process of grinding the shot. Gradually, your lovely morning pour-thick, hanging and holding out until up to two ounces before turning whitish and sickly-has become thin and finicky. Shot volumes become smaller as the flavor oils are lost to heat.

I am pleased to announce that we have solved this problem. We outfitted a grinder with a silent running computer "muffin fan," mounted in the rear of the

POWER VENT IN COFFEE GRINDER

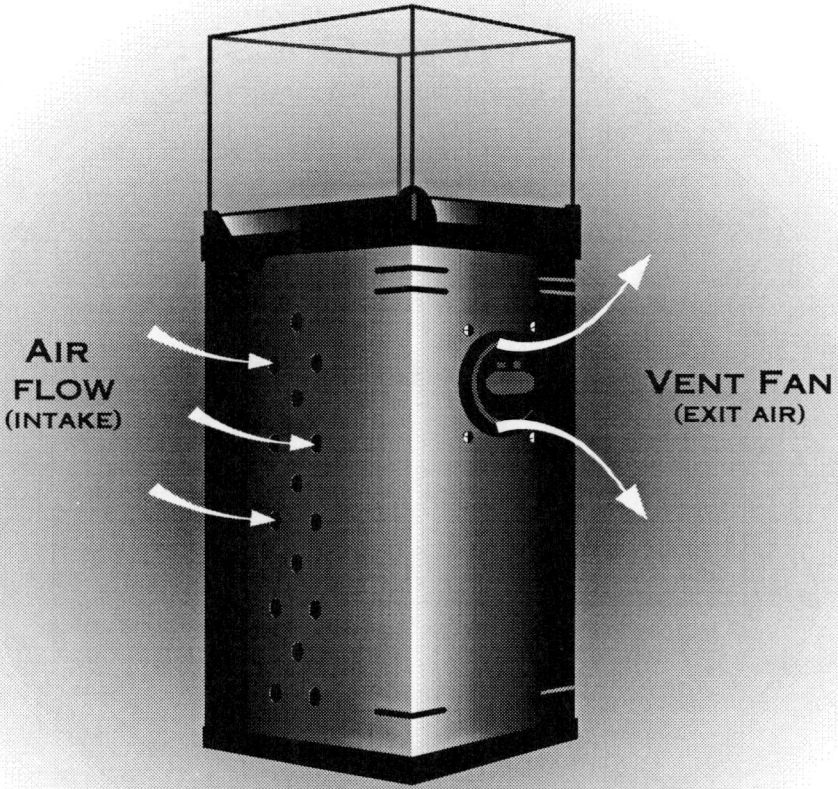

AIR
FLOW
(INTAKE)

VENT FAN
(EXIT AIR)

Venting motor heat away from grinding chamber.

case. The fan is on whenever the grinder is plugged in, and the machine runs cool regardless of volume of coffee served.

(A note on the vent fan: it tends to suck fine ground coffee into the motor housing and may require vacuuming out the interior of the grinders weekly.)

As far as wearing out switches, stock adequate replacement parts. Ditto for the moving parts of the dosing hopper.

If you decide to vent a grinder in this fashion, be sure a professional machinist installs the fan for you and cuts additional vent holes to admit additional air. In addition, get the wiring done by a professional electronics technician. The commercial espresso bar is no environment for an amateur "do-it-yourself" mindset.

V
THE ESPRESSO MACHINE

WHO WILL REPAIR IT?

Many people who attend my business seminar try to pin me down by asking, "Which espresso machine is the best?" That's when I usually quip something like "The one that works, of course." This response, however, is more serious than it may sound at first, because it contains the first elements of my real, more in-depth answer.

Before you purchase a machine for your business, investigate the technical support and parts inventory that are available for machines sold in your part of the country. If your machine breaks at 7 o'clock on Sunday morning, who will repair it? We always run two machines in each shop to address this, and we are surrounded by good repair technicians in Seattle. (One good idea when you bring in a new machine to an area is to contact your local independent technician and ask if they would be willing to go and study with the manufacturer in exchange for a service contract with your store: in other words, negotiate.)

If you are handy with light mechanical tasks and decide to take on a minor repair, ask your dealer if they will support your efforts by supplying parts and telephone troubleshooting services. If your dealer will not tell you how to adjust and maintain your own machine, as well as provide parts, find another dealer.

ABOUT THE MACHINES THEMSELVES

The characteristics needed in an espresso machine are:

1. To deliver water at *a consistent temperature* to the coffee, regardless of volume of coffee served.

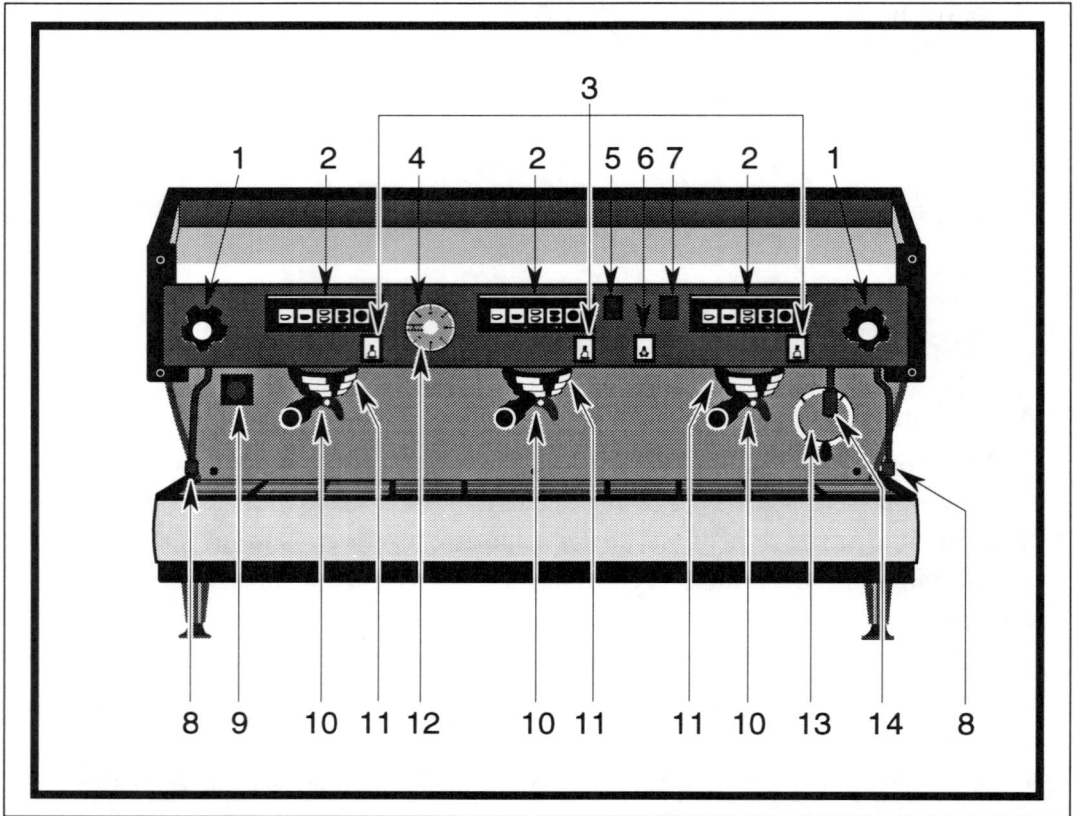

1. Steam Valve
2. Volumetric Dosing Pad
3. Semi Automatic Overrider Switch
4. Boiler Pressure Gauge
5. Heating Indicator Light
6. Manual Fill
7. Hot Water Dispensing Switch
8. Steam Wand
9. On/Off Switch
10. Portafilter
11. Group Head
12. Pump Pressure Gauge
13. Water Level Sight Glass
14. Hot Water Nozzle

Espresso machine terminology, courtesy of La Marzocco.

2. Machines must feature stable pump pressure throughout the brewing cycle.

3. The espresso machine must feature a pre-infusion cycle.

4. Steam must be of a consistent pressure and dryness, and the machine must feature user-friendly controls.

CONSISTENT TEMPERATURE

1. To deliver water at a *consistent temperature* to the coffee, regardless of volume of coffee served.

Let's break this statement down.

As I will detail in *Chapter VII: Brewing Water Temperature,* control of the temperature at the head of the machine is the greatest challenge facing the espresso engineers. Two schools of design exist to address the problem: heat exchange machines with a single large boiler; or espresso machines with two boilers, one for steam and one dedicated to brewing water only.

The basic problems you face trying to stabilize brewing water temperature include the metal diffusion blocks located on the bottom of the group head. This is the surface that brewing water spreads over before going through the dispersion screen and onto the top of the packed coffee inside the porta-filter. Being on the bottom, they are the coolest part because heat rises. In addition, being made of metal (usually brass) they radiate heat very quickly when the porta-filter is removed to brew a shot. (Diffusion blocks can be made of stainless steel, which will exchange heat with the atmosphere more slowly than brass.) You address this problem by running brewing water over them just before you lock in the porta-filter to brew a shot (See "Temperature Surfing" in *Brewing Water Temperature* chapter of this book.) Combined with the instability built into the machines we see quite a range of brewing water temperatures on the coffee bed.

The severity of the problems created by this combination greatly depends upon how busy your shop is. Heat exchange machines tend to heat up at the head while sitting idle. Espresso machines that feature a dedicated boiler may cool down a few degrees under the same conditions.

Heat exchange technologies were developed in the late 1950s by Italian engineers who wanted fresher water by quickly heating small amounts on demand. Essentially, the steam boiler is used to heat the brewing water for extraction. Most

Italian water is relatively high in mineral content which leads to scale build-up in the boilers. Water filtration also was not well developed in this era, but modern water filtration systems, combined with nickel linings in espresso boilers, have eliminated the concern of "stale water" sitting in the tank.

Alternatively, espresso machines exist with a boiler dedicated to brewing water. These machines feature temperature adjustment capability independent of steam pressure. At the time of this writing I have not discovered an espresso machine that offers greater stability of temperature at the head than one with a dedicated boiler for brewing water. It would seem to be the superior technology for temperature control.

PID Machines

PID means proportional, integral, and derivative control programs built into one process controller. In our case, the process is controlling a water boiler. Proportional means that the closer you are to the target temperature, the smaller the amount of time that the heating element is turned on. Integral and derivative programs are designed to reduce the instances of over-shooting your target temperature.

Machines advertising PID control will be superior to any alternative in regards to temperature stability if the following criteria are addressed:

1. They feature a dedicated boiler for brewing water.

2. They accurately pre-heat the water entering the brewing water boiler to within a few degrees of the operating temperature of the boiler.

3. They feature a group-head design that brings all that wonderful stability to the coffee bed.

Stable Pump Pressure

2. Machines must feature stable pump pressure throughout the brewing cycle.

There are basically two pump options in modem machines: A rotary pump or a hydraulically driven piston that magnifies incoming water pressure to the required 9 atmospheres. The drawback with the hydraulic piston is that it wastes water by requiring close to a quart of water just to achieve pressure with each shot you make. For this reason, the rotary pump seems like a better option for most locations.

I do not recommend the old piston lever machines where the operator pulls a handle to achieve pressure because many of these old designs are not very good at delivering consistent pressure. Also, in a high volume environment, the staff will have trouble with carpal tunnel syndrome, a painful and often debilitating condition associated with overuse of the wrist joint. In high-volume espresso making wrist, elbow, and shoulder problems can be caused by piston lever machines.

PRE-INFUSION CYCLE

3. The espresso machine must feature a pre-infusion cycle.

Espresso coffee likes to be saturated with brewing water just before pressurized water slams into it to provide the main extraction of the flavor. This is called pre-infusion, and should last for 1 to 2 seconds. On a machine with adequate pre-infusion, the espresso takes from 5 to 8 seconds to appear at the spout after the brewing switch is thrown.

Pre-infusion is important for two reasons. First, it loosens up the soluble flavor oils a bit and allows for more flavor to be released from the coffee. Second, it acts in a mechanical way to help seal the top of the coffee so that pressurized water does not just blast a pit in the top of the coffee through which the pressurized water escapes without doing its job.

CONSISTENT STEAM PRESSURE/DRYNESS AND USER FRIENDLY CONTROLS

4. Steam must be of a consistent pressure and dryness, and the machine must feature user-friendly controls.

Detailed steaming technique will be covered in *Chapter XVIII: Milk Texturing and Presentation.* As it pertains to machine design, however, you need to know that the quality of milk texture is quite affected by the dryness of the steam used.

Steam dryness is a function of the amount of vapor space in the main steam boiler. The best steam quality for texturing is found when the water level is just over half a tank when looking in your steam boiler sight glass (see photograph on previous page). When the liquid water rises to about 2/3 of the volume shown in the sight glass, too much moisture is in the steam.

All modem espresso machines feature automatic filling mechanisms to main-

Steam boiler sight glass—water level just over half way gives best steam quality.

To raise steam boiler pressure, turn pressure-stat counter-clockwise.

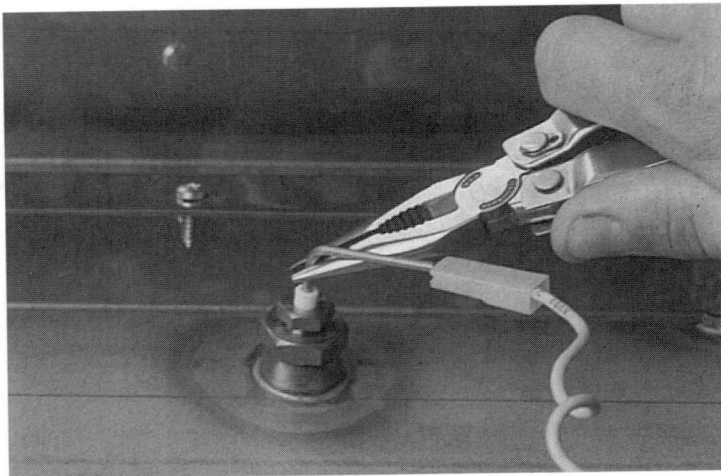

To raise water level in steam boiler, ease probe out a bit.

tain the steam boiler level. Experiment with a machine before purchasing to see if it refills often enough to maintain a relatively stable ratio between vapor and liquid or if it has large variations before filling.

Most machines use a probe mounted in the top of the steam boiler to determine vapor level. In my experience, such a system is very good at maintaining consistent water levels and is easy for the operator to adjust.

To set liquid level higher, and decrease vapor space, simply slide the probe out a bit. To lower the level of the water in the sight glass, push the probe in a bit. The tip of the probe determines the level of the water.

SEMIAUTOMATIC VS. AUTOMATIC DOSING MACHINES

My staff and I are dinosaurs. We still prefer semiautomatic espresso machines. Bless my machine importer, Kent Bakke, for special ordering our machines with this seemingly outdated technology.

What is a semiautomatic machine? It is simply one where the operator turns the pump on and off, controlling the all-important shot volume on a shot by shot basis.

An automatic dosing machine features a programmable key pad on the front. The owner or *macchinesti* (the Italian term for the espresso quality control technician) sets up desired shot volumes by programming the key pad. The program simply shuts off the pump when the desired shot volume is achieved. This technology offers greater quality control in high volume shops and mixed use environments such as restaurants, and in any location where staff turnover is high or people are not adequately trained.

Fully automatic espresso machines grind and pack the coffee, steam the milk and dispense a ready-made espresso-based beverage for you.

Oh, please, just buy a Coke or chew caffeine pills.

We Americans so often bury the romance of life in an attempt to be efficient. Although you bought this book for technique, let me state that I value the coffee shop to bring people together. Coffee and cultural development are old friends. It may be just my dinosaur leanings, but I value the human contact in going out for coffee.

Technically, an automatic machine will do a better job with the espresso than an untrained operator, but these machines are no match for the skilled barista.

The principle failures of these engineering marvels are in keeping a consistent extraction rate and milk texturing.

FINALLY, CHECK USER-FRIENDLINESS

Are there gauges for extraction pressure and boiler pressure? There should be, and they should be easy to read. Do steamer wands and controls seem easy to use and well placed? Do controls and switches seem durable or tinny? If you already have an experienced staff, enlist their help in evaluating user-friendliness of the machine.

What this chapter adds up to is this: *Instead of looking for a certain brand because someone recommended it, you need to evaluate machine choices using the aforementioned parameters.* Most of the good companies are constantly improving their designs. By knowing what is behind design choices, you are making your critical decision for yourself and are less likely to get lost in the high gloss blitz of marketing brochures.

VI
PUMP PRESSURE

One of the tricky truths about making coffee is that roasted coffee contains not only the heavenly aromatic flavors, but other compounds that are not so tasty. Before the turn of this century, the Italians correctly concluded that coffee flavor oils could be separated more efficiently from these foul tasting compounds if the water for brewing was pressurized.

Pressure serves to foam up the flavor oils into a dense reddish brown foam called crema. This crema traps very light and delicate flavors for enjoyment in the cup. The question is, "What pressure is optimum?" There is wide agreement that the pump for espresso making should be set between *8.2 and 9 atmospheres (called "bars") of pressure.* My personal choice is for 8.2 bars of pump pressure.

STABILIZING PUMP PRESSURE

At Vivace Broadway we noticed that the water pressure coming into our pump was varying widely throughout the day. In the morning, it would be higher than the afternoon, with spikes occurring irregularly. Even our washing machine would affect the front bar when it was filling.

As incoming water pressure changed, the output of our rotary pump would change with it. We solved the problem with a static-tank reservoir. Our static tank is basically a stainless steel holding tank with an automatic refill valve so that the espresso machine pump would always have incoming water at one bar, or around 15 pounds of pressure.

Various configurations will work for a simple tank to serve as a brewing water reservoir. The tank should be made of stainless steel, be easy to clean, and have at

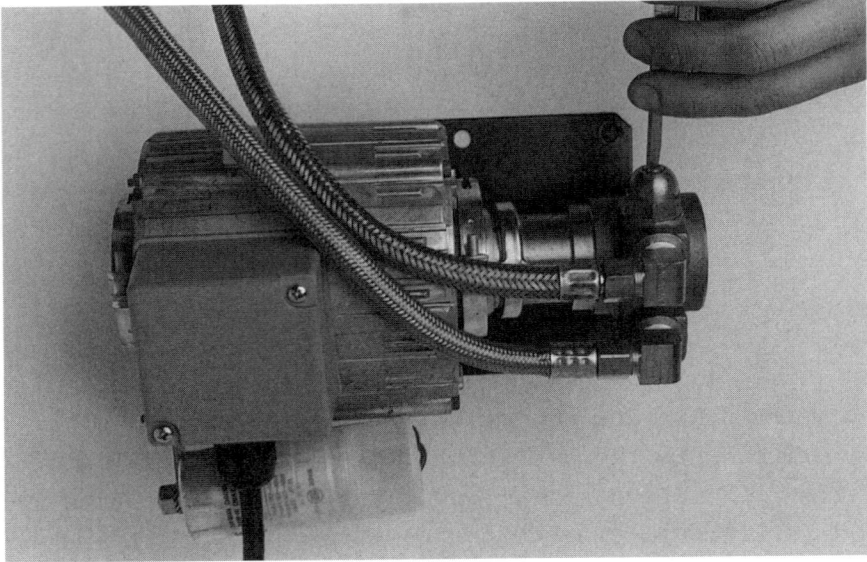

Adjust pump pressure during extraction to between 8.2 and 9 bars.

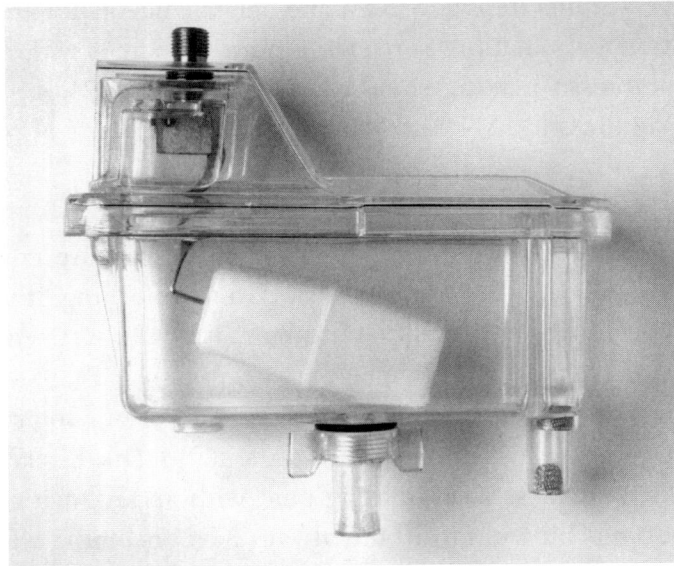

Simple liquid level control valve will keep static tank filled automatically.

least one-gallon capacity. To provide automatic refill, I suggest a liquid level control valve such as the one pictured on page 48, mounted within a your larger tank. When utilizing an inexpensive valve such as this one, be sure you have a run-off hose positioned near the top of the tank. This way when the valve fails and locks open, the excess water can be diverted to a floor drain until you notice it.

ADJUSTING YOUR PUMP PRESSURE

Rotary pumps are fitted with easy access adjustment screws. Be sure you adjust the pressure while brewing a shot. Pressure should be between 8.2 and 9.0 bar during extraction of espresso.

VII
Brewing Water Temperature
The Essence Of Quality In The Cup

The better you become at making espresso, the more that the factor of brewing water temperature will emerge as the final vexing problem. Brewing water temperature is a very difficult factor to control. But its control is essential to quality espresso making, because water temperature plays such an integral role in the preservation of coffee's volatile flavor compounds. Water temperature is responsible for the *quality and quantity* of flavors in the espresso coffee.

Water at temperatures over 200 degrees Fahrenheit and in small quantities, such as an espresso machine is designed to produce, is hard to measure. This problem is complicated by the fact that the mere act of measuring water temperature can in itself lower the water temperature by varying amounts. It's the old problem of your subject being affected by your measurement techniques.

For this reason, I recommend tasting and examining your espresso, rather than trying to measure the water temperature to determine if the brewing temperature is right. Another reason to let your taste buds guide you is that different degrees of roast may taste better at different brewing temperatures.

That being said, I will still refer to temperatures in the accompanying flavor chart and in this text to give you a general idea of the playing field. (All measurements have been made with a Fluke 51 K/J digital thermometer using a K-type, thermocouple bead probe. The degree of roast features beans a deep mahogany brown with no visible oils on the surface.)

Symptoms Of Temperature Problems

If your extraction water temperature is changing during brewing, and is averaging less than 206 degrees Fahrenheit, the color of the crema is a light cinnamon brown. The espresso will be a bland mish-mash of flavors with no varietal flavors, or caramelized sugars, in the cup. The beautiful red-brown espresso crema is only produced when brewing temperatures are stable within a two-degree range during the elapsed time for the shot as it is made. It is possible for caffe espresso to have beautiful red-brown crema, but still taste perfectly hideous. The stability of temperature gives you the beautiful crema color, but only when brewing temperature is stable (within one degree of error) and set at about 203.5 degrees Fahrenheit (at sea level) will you achieve a sweet tasting espresso, with a full bouquet of varietal aromas.

BREWING WATER TEMPERATURE GRAPH

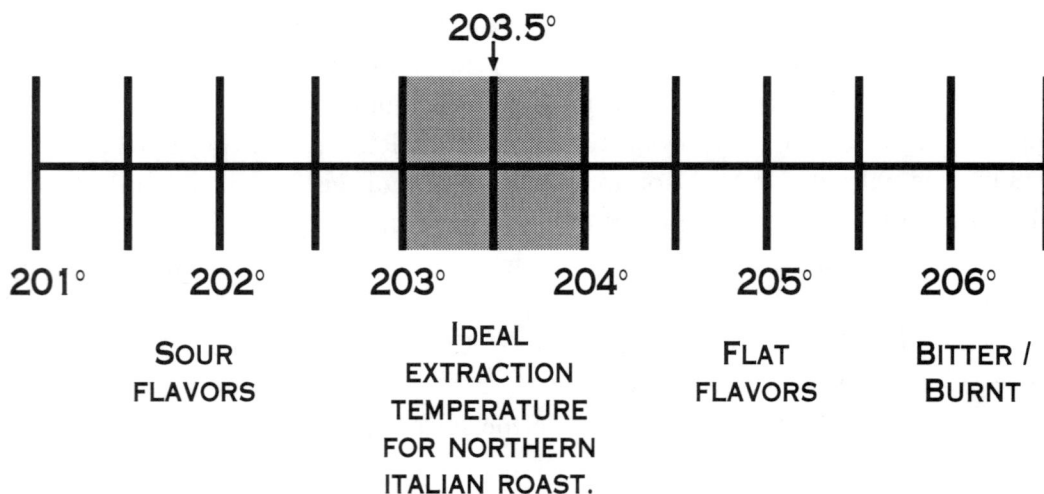

203.5°

201°	202°	203°	204°	205°	206°
	SOUR FLAVORS	IDEAL EXTRACTION TEMPERATURE FOR NORTHERN ITALIAN ROAST.		FLAT FLAVORS	BITTER / BURNT

Low Water Temperatures

Perhaps the most extreme sin using my roast is slightly low brewing water temperature, say from 199 to 202 degrees F. **Low temperature brewing will produce sour espresso using a Northern Italian Roast** such as mine. Brewing with lower water temperature, say 192 to 199 degrees F., will produce espresso that is bland with a parchment flavor and no sweetness.

High Water Temperature

On the other hand, **over-temperature brewing water will burn the coffee oils**, and the espresso will feature a mid-tongue bite and a burnt after-taste. Heavy, dark streaking will appear on the crema and it will have large bubbles in the foam structure* in the extreme case. Water that is slightly over temperature will merely flatten out the flavors and create an inoffensive but boring caffe espresso.

Perfect Brewing Water Temperature

When water temperature is held between 203 and 204 degrees F. at sea level during the brewing of a shot, all the sugars can come out and play. The flavor profile of the espresso (roasted to the Northern Italian color) features a heavy caramel sweetness, with varietal flavors emerging in the after taste—earthy chocolate from Ethiopian, floral aromas from fine Cerrado Brazils, hints of anise, and a crispy toast-crust flavor from the roast itself. Control of all the factors, combined with perfect temperature during extraction, finally can elevate caffe espresso to the very top of the pantheon of brewing methods for the much beleaguered coffee bean. After five centuries of research, the espresso method can deliver a flavor/aroma sensation in your mouth that is the closest to the fragrance of the fresh ground blend.

---

*(Sweet espresso made with temperatures varying less than one degree F. may also feature some large bubbles in the crema within a beautiful red-brown color. I think the preservation of so much caramelized sugar during brewing gives a light and fragile chiffon texture to the crema. It is extraordinary in its delicate, silky mouth-feel but does not last as long as crema that is less sweet.)

The appearance of the crema is a deep brown with reddish highlights as the cup is swirled. As I mentioned above, the crema of truly sweet espresso is lighter in body and fragile compared to less sweet, but well prepared caffe espresso. As with all things in life, it seems that the sweetest caffe espresso is also the most fragile and must only be enjoyed at the bar in a heavy porcelain cup of the right shape and size. Please refer to the color photographs on pages 108 and 109 for a guide to color.

Brewing at High Altitude

Brewing caffe espresso at higher altitudes than sea level requires lower brewing temperature. If you are in Denver, Colorado, the mile high city, you are just going to have to experiment to find your ideal brewing temperature. Espresso brewed at that altitude will appear the same as burnt espresso brewed at too high a temperature; dark, streaky with a lot of big bubbles in the crema. At this time I am not sure if a Northern Italian roast can be made to taste sweet at such an altitude.

As I mentioned in Chapter V: Espresso Machines in the first edition of this book, this factor is the Holy Grail of espresso machine design. It gives me no end of pleasure that as I type this, for the first time in the history of caffe espresso, stable machines are available. The first design to achieve temperature stability sufficient to preserve the caramelized sugars through brewing has been made by the TREUH Company in Seattle. Engineer Mark Barnett has released the fragrance of coffee from its prison of mediocrity with his brilliant dual PID controlled espresso machine.

Using the new PID machines, however, is even more an artistic endeavor than older technology. The role of the barista as a culinary artist is enhanced by temperature stabilized equipment. It is true that he or she can create perfect espresso (remember, perfect means it very closely tastes like the fragrance of the roasted coffee) but it remains quite tricky to do so. Perhaps flow rate has become even more critical—fast pours are more sour and slow pours are degraded due to burning the coffee oils and sugars. And, with perfection possible, any problem with your program is much more destructive to the potential of your espresso.

Searching for the heart of the espresso flavor is analogous to searching for a diamond in a pitch-black gymnasium. With the old machines, it was like search-

ing with a flashlight. Pretty easy to find the diamond, but when your broad beam of light struck the jeweled surface of the stone it was no big deal, just a flash of light. Using the new PID machines you are searching with a laser beam. It may be much more difficult to find the diamond, but when the laser strikes it, the full beauty of the gem is revealed.

One source of temperature instability is still present. The group head cools down when the porta-filter is removed. For this reason, activating the pump for two seconds just before brewing the shot (temperature surfing) is critical to real-ize the stability built into a PID machine. And, as always, porta-fil-ters must be locked into the group-head during use of the machine.

Temperature control is the rea-son that the porta-filter is always kept in the group-head of the machine. These brewing baskets should never rest on the counter or the top of the machine during busi-ness hours. If you see the porta-fil-ters lying on the drain tray when a shop is open and serving espresso on that machine, forget it. Go some-where else for an espresso.

SETTING YOUR TARGET TEMPERATURE

It is not possible to use a stem thermometer for measuring espresso machine water. It will be necessary to invest in a digital thermometer with a high-speed, low mass bead probe such as the Fluke 51. It is a matter of accuracy and speed of measurement. If you can get your hands on such a thermometer, here is how I measure my brewing water temperature.

By placing the thermocouple (the little bead) in the packed coffee itself, you

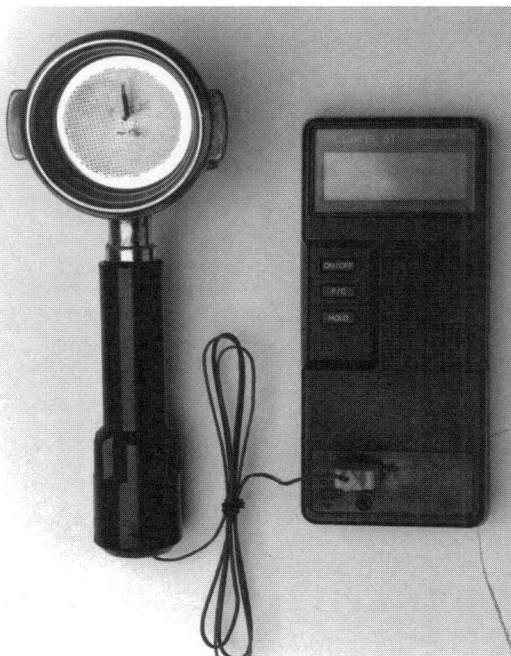

Note the tiny thermocouple positioned near the top of coffee basket.

can monitor brewing water temperature as you are pulling a shot. This is the ideal situation. Be sure to put the bead close to the top of the packed coffee. Keep the hole that admits the probe into the coffee basket as small as possible. The packed coffee will seal the wire into the basket. Pretty neat, eh?

Most heat-exchange type espresso machines accumulate heat at the head when not in use. Their resting head temperatures will be higher than the target temperature.

Espresso machines with a dedicated boiler for brewing water may have a resting head temperature three or four degrees Fahrenheit lower than the *target* temperature.

TEMPERATURE SURFING

We call the art of manipulating the head and porta-filters to stabilize brewing water temperature *temperature surfing*. It is a very sophisticated activity, separating the merely good espresso maker from the truly great coffee maestro. It is entirely intuitive, but there are some specific techniques that we use.

On the machines I have tested, a repeatable temperature is achieved after two samples (of two ounces each) have been quickly discarded from the head of the machine. The game is to be able to manipulate the machine to deliver water with a smaller range of variation at the head of the machine. The idea is to get past the resting head temperature towards your target temperature. It is crucial not to draw more than two ounces each time you "pulse" the head.

The diffusion block resides at the bottom of the group head and water delivery tubing. Obviously, this is the coolest spot in the system because heat rises. This is the primary reason we "surf the temperature" by running the brewing water through the group head just before brewing, to bring this slab of metal up to its designed brewing temperature. I call it a sophisticated technique because different machines will require different amounts of water. In addition, as the machine is used more the barista must be intuitively able to adjust his or her surfing technique to achieve the best espresso.

Being busy—using the heads constantly—aids you in creating a stable temperature at the head. Commercial espresso machines are designed for continuous use, which leads to the greatest stability of brewing water temperature.

In Italy, you rarely see an espresso bar with a machine smaller than a three group. Larger espresso machines feature more stable temperatures at the head. For pure coffee quality, machines with three group heads are the smallest I recommend for use in a bar. The greater mass of metal and hot water of the larger machines is responsible for the overall stability of brewing water temperature.

THE IMPORTANCE OF RETAINING PORTA-FILTER HEAT

If it has been a few minutes since you last made a shot of espresso, activate the pump and force two ounces of water through the porta-filter and the old coffee puck to preheat the porta-filter. Do this while grinding the shot for the customer. Note: Yes, we do leave the exhausted coffee puck in the porta-filter between orders because it contains heat of its own and will help you keep the porta-filter temperature more constant.

When you remove the porta-filter to pack the shot, be quick. Bang out the old grounds, dose and pack your coffee with rapid precision. It is a race to see how warm you can keep the porta-filter. Then, just before replacing it, pulse the head, releasing a two-ounce water sample. Then slam in the porta-filter and activate the pump without any wasted time (to review this procedure, see *Chapter XXI: Vivace Espresso Method*).

THE PERILS OF RINSING

After banging out the old coffee puck, you will see varying amounts of old grounds clinging to the basket. At Vivace, we quickly wipe it out with a dry towel (see packing section), but many people activate the group head and rinse out the grounds using brewing water. This is a mistake and can cause your espresso machine to go under your target temperature.

Espresso machines are carefully engineered to offer the greatest temperature stability while delivering little one- or two-ounce samples of brewing water. That is why I am careful to emphasize that the above pulsing method uses only small 2 ounce samples of brewing water to stabilize the head temperature. Running excess water through the head is not the best way to use these machines.

To remove coffee crusties from the brewing basket, use the hot water jet from

the steam boiler. The technique may even add additional heat to the metal of the porta-filter-something you want.

If you think you have a water temperature problem, consult your service technician on how to adjust your particular espresso machine. The vast majority of espresso machines feature a heat exchange system that is dependent on the temperature of the steam boiler.

VIII
MACHINE CLEANLINESS
NEXT TO GODLINESS

Extracted coffee oils can build up on all surfaces that come into contact with the liquid coffee. These deposited oils quickly become bitter due to the chemical instability of the flavor compounds. When your fresh espresso comes into contact with these old deposited coffee oils, the result is a rancid bite in the final cup.

The bad news is that dirty equipment is very common at many espresso making establishments in the States. The good news, however, is that there is a simple solution to the problem—diligent cleaning, followed with "seasoning."

An espresso maker must regard his or her porta-filter (see photograph) and group head much as a great chef would regard his or her sauce pan. It must be clean, yes, but it also must be seasoned with coffee oils so that the liquid espresso does not come into contact with the bare metal. For this reason, it is essential that after cleaning the porta-filter (as shown in the photograph on the following page) or backflushing with espresso detergent, a seasoning shot be made and discarded to prepare the metal surfaces for coffee making.

In this chapter, we will focus on nightly cleaning procedures and other periodic espresso machine cleaning requirements. Later, in *Chapter XVII: Cleaning Techniques,* we will discuss how to operate your espresso machine to keep the machine clean as you work.

A. PORTA-FILTERS

Remove the coffee baskets and soak your porta-filters overnight in a solution

of hot water with one tablespoon of espresso detergent dissolved in it. In the morning, scrub vigorously with a Scotch Brite® green scrubbing pad, the kind that scratches glass. Get a tiny bottle brush to reach hidden crusties in the tiny apertures on the spouts.

When soaking, do not submerge the plastic portion of the handle because over time it will be damaged by the detergent.

It will be necessary to develop a regular habit of soaking these brewing baskets every night. In this way it is easy to keep coffee oils from accumulating. If allowed to collect, coffee oil deposits can be quite difficult to dislodge from interior spouts.

When porta-filters are dirty, the appearance of the espresso will change along with the flavor. The crema will not look quite as luxurious as it oozes out of the spout. It becomes a bit ragged looking and may feature whitish stripes in with the red-brown flavor oils.

Porta-filters will also need to be scrubbed each hour that you are making coffee (please see *Chapter XVII: Cleaning Techniques*).

Clean porta-filter with blind filter and double-shot filter baskets.

B. Backflushing with Espresso Detergent

Backflushing an espresso machine means replacing your coffee basket in the handle with a blind filter, a device that looks like a coffee basket but has no holes in the bottom. The blind filter serves to build up pump pressure against it which is then released in a flushing action out the drain located behind the group head.

All modern espresso machines feature a valve and drain network to release pressurized brewing water. Otherwise, after a shot has been made, hot water and spent coffee grounds would spray all over the place when the handle is removed to make the next shot. You must have a valve to release the built up pressure. This valve and drain network is located just inside the group head behind the dispersion screen. As brewing water moves towards the coffee during extraction, it shares a common tube with the backflush system. This common tube will become rancid with accumulated coffee oils.

Espresso detergents have been developed to liquefy and remove coffee oil deposits within this tube and valve network. The active ingredient in the detergent is trisodium phosphate (TSP). Espresso machine cleaners are buffered with

From left to right: single, double and triple, baskets.

61

foaming agents and compounds to prevent TSP from attacking gaskets and softer materials within the group. They are expensive, but necessary to clean and preserve the integrity of internal valves and gaskets.

As a minimum machine cleaning schedule, backflush with espresso detergent each evening as you close up for the day. Follow the instructions on the detergent as dictated for your type of machine.

At Vivace, we use a teaspoon of espresso detergent placed in the blind filter. Secure the group handle into place in the head and activate the pump for 30 seconds. Release pressure and repeat twice for three or four-second intervals. This is the wash cycle.

After washing, it is essential to rinse the soap out of the group head before serving. Remove the blind filter and rinse it under hot water. Then run short bursts of brewing water through the head of the machine until it is clear. Put the clean blind filter back into the group. Then energize the pump for about five seconds and release, repeating this step five times. Backflushing with clear water at least five times is essential to achieve an effective rinsing.

You may find it necessary to clean the machines with detergent during the day. Taste the coffee frequently to create your own cleaning schedule. At Vivace, we clean machines after every four hours of service (see *Chapter XVII: Cleaning Techniques* for details).

C. DISPERSION SCREENS

Remove dispersion screens nightly and clean them. Clean the dispersion screw and the group head under the screen as needed (see photograph on next page).

D. GROUP GASKETS

Clean the group head gaskets with a small, stiff brush when you have the screens out. (Many machine manufacturers and reps have special brushes for this task in inventory.) These gaskets are the ones that the porta-filter snugs up against when the group handle is put into place, creating a sealed environment to contain pressurized brewing water (see photograph on next page).

Remove dispersion screws nightly.

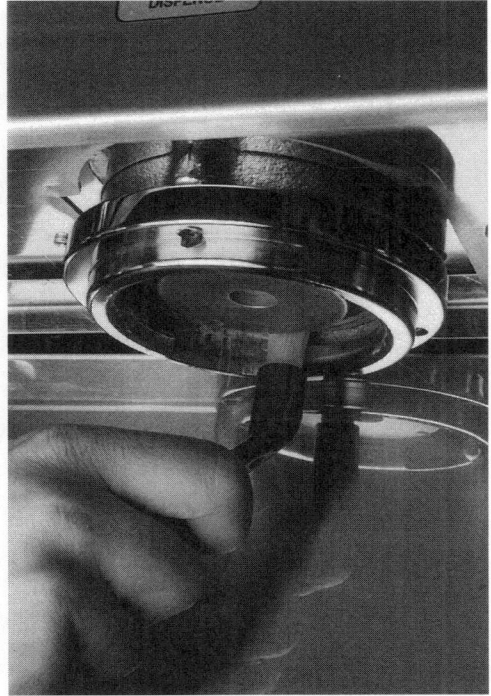

Clean gaskets and scrub machine head with Scotch Brite® pad each night at closing.

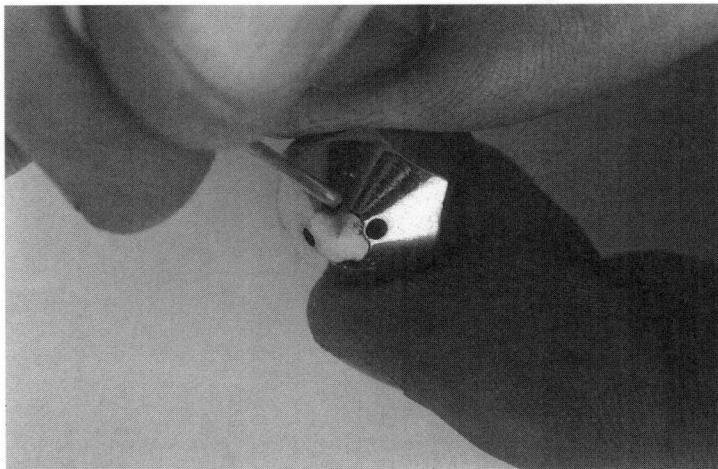

Clean steamer tips with a paper clip.

E. Group Head

There is a surface of bronze or a similar metal behind the dispersal screen. Scrub this nightly with a Scotch Brite® pad while dispersal screens are out.

F. Steamer Tips

On a nightly basis, remove steamer tips and clean apertures with a pin or brush. It may be beneficial to run a small brush up the wand as well. Many technicians recommend submerging the steamers in water overnight to soak off crusties. The problem with this is that if the power goes off in the building the boilers cool off. The cruddy water is then sucked up the steamer wand and into your steam boiler. Not a pretty picture.

These procedures, if performed by your closing crew each night, will not only help keep the coffee sweet, they also will increase the longevity and reliability of your espresso machine. Coupled with good water filtration and periodic maintenance checkups by a factory-trained technician, good cleaning habits should allow your commercial espresso machine to last indefinitely.

INGREDIENT FACTORS

IX
WATER PURITY & MINERAL CONTENT

Fortunately, we do not have to be chemical engineers to make very good espresso coffee. Some things, like water filtration, can be delegated to a specialist to handle. What you need to know from me, however, are a few basic truths.

Water that features a high mineral content, the kind that leaves an oily finish in your mouth when you drink it, is bad for your espresso machine and can adversely affect the taste of espresso coffee. Water high in minerals will cause scale build up (whitish deposits of calcium and lime) in your boilers and the water lines servicing the head of the espresso machine.

The ideal water for espresso coffee making retains about 2-3 grains of calcium and is free of chlorine and particulate contaminants. The removal of excess minerals in the water is crucial.

The filters that remove these minerals are generally called water softeners. You may or may not need much water softening in your local area. To detect it with your taste buds, check for an oily, slimy sort of taste in the back of your mouth as you drink and after you swallow. Do side-by-side tastings with a good bottled water. In addition, solicit advice from a local water purification company that is familiar with your particular water supply.

Remember, water must also be filtered for impurities other than these standard minerals, including particulate and chlorine.

Both of these purification issues can be addressed for your particular water by contacting a company that specializes in food service water filtration in your area. In Seattle, my consultant is Heathco International which sets up Everpure water filtration systems. I use a triple cold carbon filtration system with a coarse filter

on the input, three main canisters for filtration and a de-scaler on the output. The system we use costs between $800 and $1,000 installed.

Filters must be changed when they become fatigued. How long they will actually last will depend on the quality of the water. On my system, the symptom of dirty filters is a drop in available water pressure. Different filter technologies will have different symptoms when exhausted. Check with your local distributor for details.

The life cycle of the filters also will depend on diligent changing of the coarse pre-filter. Regular replacement of these cheap pre-filters is very cost effective when you consider the alternative—changing the much more pricey main canisters.

One important note is that you do not want to use "distilled" water in your espresso machine. The water level probes in most espresso machines depend on tiny conductive particles to be present in the water to function. These conductive particles are not present in distilled water.

X
COFFEE FRESHNESS
PROTECTING ROASTED COFFEE FROM AIR AND WATER

Think of whole bean coffee as you do fresh-baked bread. Under ideal storage conditions, roasted whole bean coffee remains fresh for no more than ten days after roasting. Use it or lose it in ten days. That's the rule.

In all coffee making methods, freshness is the dominant factor in creating quality in the cup. In the case of espresso, this is particularly true. Freshness of the bean is the single factor most responsible for thick crema. As the espresso comes out of the machine, you can see staleness. Stale coffee appears thin and watery compared to the thick red-brown crema of fresh coffee, which indicates optimum flavor content.

As I have repeatedly mentioned, the ability to isolate the effect of stale coffee on the appearance of the pour is dependent on having all the other factors in control. An uneven distribution and pack, or dull grinder burrs, for example, will cause the pour to also appear thin and watery.

Espresso made from beans over ten days old has less crema and creates a lighter density that is not heavy enough to hang from the spouts like it should. The espresso will suck in a bit off the bottom of the spout from surface tension.

Short-term storage techniques for coffee are similar to those used for wine. Keep coffee in a cool, dark place in sealed containers. Typically, we drop bags of coffee, fresh from the roaster, into plastic food storage cans with snap-down lids. Again, long-term storage of roasted coffee is not possible, so use it up within ten days.

If your roaster is concerned with freshness, he or she will put the date of roasting on the package of coffee you receive, a practice known as *open dating*. In addition, a good roaster will package the coffee within ten hours after roasting to make use of the CO_2 gas the beans emit. Roasted coffee will out-gas CO_2 as a by-product of the roasting, also known as a Maillard reaction (a reaction that is characterized by the production of CO_2 and caramelized sugars and is exothermic, meaning it produces energy in its final stages). As a matter of fact, fresh roasted coffee will emit 85 percent of its available CO_2 within ten hours after roasting.

The importance of this CO_2 release is that it will force air out of the package and prevent oxidation of the coffee. Exposure to the air, like opening the bag and pouring some coffee beans out a couple of times, can cause staleness in whole bean coffee literally overnight. The carbon dioxide is heavier than air and is literally poured into your grinding hopper as the beans are poured out. It acts like a liquid. (Like so many things in espresso, the actual life of whole bean coffee exposed to air is a function of other variables such as air temperature and humidity. High temperatures and low humidity greatly accelerate oxidation.)

SWISS WATER DECAF AND FRESHNESS

We blend varieties of Swiss Water Decaf beans to achieve a decaffeinated espresso that is truly wonderful when it is fresh. This blend features a very thick texture and a mellow flavor similar to our regular blends.

The catch is that the process used to decaffeinate the beans breaks down the internal cell walls of the coffee beans. This allows for accelerated osmosis of flavor compounds to the surface of the bean. We see oil appearing on the Decaf beans within four days after roasting, given storage conditions similar to the regular bean.

After oils begin appearing on the surface of the bean, the loss of crema in the cup is quite rapid, as soon as five days after roasting. With this in mind, I recommend that you ask your roaster to package your decaf in 1/2-pound bags, drop the bags in a sealed container and refrigerate for a ten-day shelf life.

The Refrigeration/Freezing Rap

The other natural enemy of roasted coffee is water. Water on the beans seems to coagulate the flavor oils. Coffee so afflicted could jam your grinder. This pertains to refrigeration or freezing because cold beans, brought out

suddenly into your warm espresso cafe, will instantly form a layer of water on them through the action of condensation. If you refrigerate, bring the containers out into the room a few hours before use. They must be at room temperature before opening to prevent condensation from forming.

Ironically, roasted coffee itself carries within it a certain amount of moisture that is very important to the preservation of coffee flavors. Refrigerators and freezers are very dry environments and they can attack your beans' internal moisture through the action of desiccation or rapid evaporation. This rapid flight of the water from the bean strips out volatile flavor oils along with it. The solution to this is to put the unopened coffee bags into sealed containers before refrigeration.

If you want to pin me down, okay, I never refrigerate my regular blends. We do refrigerate the decaf due to its extreme volatility after roasting. We put it into 1/2 pound bags and each bag is put into a container before refrigeration. The decaf is fine for up to a week after roasting if refrigerated right after roasting.

Ground Coffee

Grinding coffee exposes most of the volatile flavor oils to the air as it is being ground. With all of this exposure, oxidation can begin immediately, robbing you of valuable flavor. For this reason, we always grind each shot to order. No pre-grinding is allowed. This is not a subtle distinction. Grinding per order is going to give you a vastly superior espresso over grinding in advance.

As a practical matter, during times of moderate humidity and temperatures about 60/60—ground coffee may last up to 4 minutes after grinding. When it's hot and dry, however, we see deterioration in the coffee in a matter of a few seconds.

XI
CHOOSING AN ESPRESSO ROAST & BLEND

ROASTING DEGREE

I am very opinionated in this area, which, of course, is the beauty of the world of coffee. Everyone is opinionated, and passionate (hopefully) about their personal taste.

I believe that espresso coffee tastes best when the bean is roasted to a deep mahogany brown with the roasting process stopped before the oils are forced out to the surface of the bean. This level of roast fully develops the natural caramelized sugars produced in the bean during roasting. The result, at best, is a sweet espresso coffee perfectly balanced with a hint of roasty nuttiness.

Speaking of taste, the rule of thumb is to please yourself. It is your shop and it should reflect what you personally think is the best. People will tell you that you must use this or you must use that because it is popular, etc., but I urge you to follow your own muse and never pander to what someone else describes as the "market."

Choosing an espresso roast is a stylistic endeavor, but allow me one objective comment relating to coffee oils. A fresh, dark roast features a shiny bean, almost black in color. If the bean is shiny right after roasting, what is it that shines? It is, of course, the coffee oils. The flavor oils. Continued exposure to heat gives a dark roast its black color and forces flavor oils out of the bean.

If these oils are on the outside of the bean, where they are exposed to air, they quickly will become rancid due to oxidation. These rancid oils will contribute a bitter bite in the cup, and there is less coffee flavor left in the bean to extract, which means less crema. It is my personal preference, then, to keep as

much of these precious oils as possible inside the bean throughout the roasting process.

Darker roasts provide more roasting flavor, like a nutty bite when mixed with milk, that some people really like. As a straight espresso these dark roasts feature an intense bitterness. The bitter roasted flavor has completely overcome and obliterated the subtle varietal tones. the coffee beans contain. The French style *caffe au lait* is based on this style of coffee being served at breakfast in a bowl of milk. Personally, I don't need a bowl of milk everyday. I just want an espresso coffee that tastes good.

In Italy, where espresso culture has developed in the last one hundred years, there are limitless stylistic nuances available in the espresso roast. Let's look at the three broad trends.

Northern Italian Roast

A Northern Italian roast is one where the beans are a deep chocolate or mahogany brown with no oils on the surface. *Illy Caffe* of Trieste, Italy, perhaps the finest of the Italian roasting and blending companies, calls this degree of roasting *normale,* or normal. In this tradition, regional variations in different beans from around the world are highlighted. All of the coffee nuances are preserved within the coffee beans and none are destroyed. The actual flavor of roasted material, the bitter bite, is not a dominant element in the final cup. It exists in balance with the more subtle coffee flavors.

The danger for the roaster is that some beans, particularly from Central and South America, will contribute too much acidity in the final cup. Excessive acid in the blend can be like an eraser, wiping out many of the sweeter flavors as the espresso is extracted. Remember, as you roast darker, acidity decreases and bitterness increases. There is a balance that needs to be achieved.

The Northern Italian roast will also be finicky for the barista making espresso coffee. Low extraction temperatures will make this roast taste sour. Espresso machines will need to be set at around 203 degrees Fahrenheit at the head to avoid this problem. Any rancid oils on the group handles will cause this coffee to taste bitter, so the Northern Italian barista must be very diligent on *machine cleaning.*

Northern Italian roasts can be considered the virtuoso espresso tradition,

offering the richest and sweetest flavors in the world of espresso, but only if prepared with great care.

CENTRAL ITALIAN ROAST

Continuing the roasting process, we find a degree of roast typified by espresso found in Florence, Italy. Beans roasted a darker brown with a light sheen of oil on the surface.

In the finished cup of espresso, the most subtle of the coffee flavors are lost. They are either dominated by the flavor of the roast or destroyed by the roasting process itself. In the Central Italian style of espresso, the bite of the roasting flavor is more present in the espresso. Also, a little less flavor is available because flavor oils, having been extruded out onto the surface of the bean, are lost by exposure to the air. Espresso ristretto in Central Italy may be served at less than 3/4 of an ounce total volume.

SOUTHERN ITALIAN ROAST

South of Naples, I found coffee beans roasted to a very dark brown with heavy oil deposits on the outside of the bean.

Nearly black coffee beans, all shiny with their precious oils glistening on the surface, look great in the bin, don't they? They just reek richness and seem to promise an orgasmic coffee experience.

Alas, in my opinion, it is but the song of the siren.

In truth, they are shiny because continued roasting has caused them to "sweat out" most of their flavor oils. Indeed, much of the varietal nuance of the coffee is destroyed by the prolonged exposure to heat and higher peak temperatures during the roasting process.

What's left? Roasting flavor itself is what is left, and caffeine, of course. In espresso making, dark roast features a burnt rubber taste in the finished cup of coffee. It is always loaded down with sugar if it is to be drunk straight, and pulled very short. In Naples, along the Via Roma, espresso ristretto is served at about 1/2 an ounce. The tazzina (small ceramic cups) are kept in hot water baths next to the machine so that they are at the exact temperature of the espresso. This

ensures that even the smallest volume of red-brown crema will survive long enough to be enjoyed.

(It should be noted that all roasting degrees found in Italy are medium to dark compared to the world spectrum. Many Northern European cultures enjoy acidic, very lightly roasted coffee beans made in a drip cone or plunger pot coffee method. Please see color photograph on page 107.)

BLENDING

Any good espresso coffee will be composed of more than one type of coffee, mixed together to provide a full flavor balance. Single coffees tend to offer a limited esthetic balance and do not provide a complex taste and aftertaste, in the form of true caffe espresso. Again, these are purely stylistic choices, but in this area there is wide agreement from roasters of all styles of espresso.

Naturally, there is vigorous disagreement on the best bean varieties to use for caffe espresso. Two species of plant produce beans we roast and then call coffee: *coffea arabica* and *coffea robusta.* Coffea arabica is the high grown, low caffeine coffee plant, considered to have more subtle and rich flavor potential. Coffea robusta is a hardier plant. It is easier to grow at lower altitudes and features a higher caffeine content than its finicky cousin, coffea arabica.

Many traditional Italian roasters feel that an espresso blend is not complete without the addition of the robusta bean. In fact, the robusta bean may constitute up to 40% of some Italian blends. American gourmet roasters do not use robusta, considering it to have an inferior flavor, often described as woody with an oily mouth feel. Nearly all marketing, advertising and point-of-purchase campaigns in the U.S. highlight the use of "all arabica" blends.

With this distinction made, it should be noted that coffee grown in different climates and soils will have very different character and aroma in the cup. The rich, chocolate body of properly roasted Ethiopian Mocha Harrar makes this one of the world's premier varietal coffees. Many Brazilian coffees offer a mild richness that some find to be an excellent basis for an espresso blend.

If you are trying to blend a Northern Italian espresso coffee, you must pay particular attention to choose only coffees naturally low in acidity. Continued roasting will reduce acidity, but the caramelized sugars will be masked by the

roasting bite. So for the "caramel" coffee, you have no choice but to select low acid varietals.

Blending, therefore, can be a complex matter and a whole world in itself. Roasters will guard their recipes with the same ferocity of a great French chef protecting what he or she sees as the "soul" of their particular cuisine. To study the art of blending, I recommend a hands-on approach like tasting excursions through Northern Italy with a very important stop at the world famous *Illy Caffe* in Treiste.

COMPARING COFFEES

To compare coffees, start with the aroma. The rich aroma of the coffee should find its way into in the cup with a good espresso barista. Aroma is a coffee's signature and marks its potential. To fully understand the coffee's aroma, smell the beans in the bag and then grind some and smell the fresh ground coffee.

To compare the taste of two or more coffees you must brew them both under standardized conditions. It is essential to minimize the number of variables in the brewing process to avoid errors in preparation that might not give you a true comparison. For this reason, do not compare coffees using the espresso method because, as this whole book has shown, espresso technique is a maze of interrelated variables.

Coffee professionals use a technique called cupping, the essence of which is brewing coffee with the fewest number of variables in the process.

Here is the cupping method I was taught.

1. Grind a seven-gram sample of coffee.

2. Bring some fresh (not previously boiled) purified drinking water just to a boil, in an enamel-lined tea pot.

3. Put the ground coffee into a preheated four-ounce cup and pour the water over it.

4. Let the mixture stand for five minutes, stirring once at two minutes.

5. Taste the coffee using a spoon and aspirate it into a mist in your mouth by slurping forcefully.

6. Evaluate flavors for acidity, strength, character, sweetness and bitterness.

A professional cupper could write an entire book on the above method. Suffice it to say that you are trying to treat each coffee exactly the same.

For example, it is crucial that water be brought just to a boil. Prolonged boiling robs water of oxygen which will affect the coffee. Each sample must be of a uniform grind and grinding must occur exactly at the same time relative to immersion in the water.

Each sample should be of identical freshness, preferably four days after roasting, given proper storage.

So cupping presents a host of variables in itself. Coffee is tricky, volatile stuff. Do not, however, forget a most important variable—you. Remember that caffeine is a drug and can affect the way you perform and what you taste, especially over a period of prolonged cupping. When the body has had enough caffeine, even the finest coffee will taste bad. Your body is warning you—enough is enough. When cupping or comparing coffees in any form, swish and spit. Don't swallow.

Relating characteristics found in cupping to the espresso method is a matter of experience. Coffee will taste differently made as espresso due to its concentration. Many subtle flavors are below the threshold of detection in the cupping method. These subtleties, however, are free to come out and play a role in the quality—or lack of quality—in the espresso. The more you understand these subtle characteristics, the better you will get at enticing them out of the bean.

Techniques of the Barista

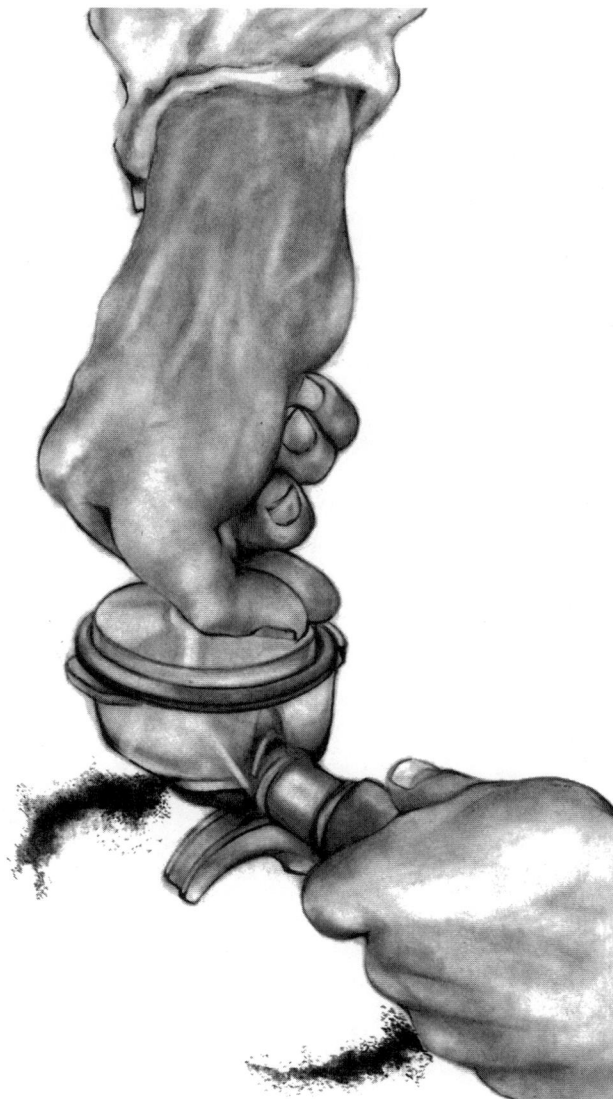

XII
ESPRESSO PACKING
TOOLS AND TECHNIQUES

I took my first espresso packing lesson from La Marzocco importer Kent Bakke in Seattle during the fall of 1987. Kent was an intense sort of packer. After grinding the coffee, he'd hunch over the porta-filter like an arm wrestler gearing up to do battle. With his hand firmly gripping the porta-filter's small black handle, he'd begin tamping the coffee and banging the sides of the group with such force that I was poised to call 911 in case he slipped. His hand would be instantly crushed.

Through clenched teeth, Kent patiently explained that espresso coffee had to be packed down hard to be "real" espresso. He told me it was "The Italian Way." He was right, of course, but it would take me years to articulate the reasons why.

Take a look at the diagrams on the next page—cutaway pictures of a coffee basket. This is the ideal situation: the coffee is evenly distributed before packing and then firmly packed. The coffee is level and of a consistent density which will force the brewing water to flow through evenly, coaxing out every drop of flavor from the ground coffee.

You must pack the ground espresso coffee so that the brewing water, which is under 120 pounds of force from the pump, does not find a sneaky way through the wafer of coffee. Water is lazy stuff. Given a choice, it will take the *path of least resistance*. Coffee packed too softly can be blasted out of the way by pressurized water which creates a pit in the surface of the coffee (see Diagram 2). The water goes down the pit. This will rob you of the flavors locked in the surrounding coffee.

Also, packing hard allows the use of a more coarse grind setting which min-

IDEALIZED EXTRACTION SERIES

1   LOOSE GROUND COFFEE.

2   EVENLY DISTRIBUTED AND DOSED.

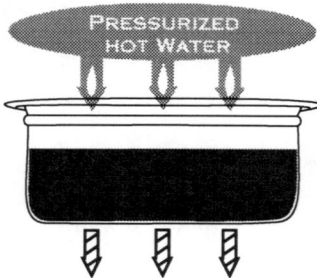

3   HARD PACKED & POLISHED.

PRESSURIZED HOT WATER

PERFECT EVEN EXTRACTION.

ONLY A PERFECT DISTRIBUTION, PACK AND POLISH CREATE AN EVEN RESISTANCE TO HOT, PRESSURIZED WATER.

SOFT PACKING: THE PROBLEM OF PITTING

(1) LOOSE GROUND
COFFEE.

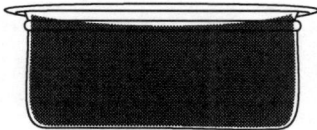

(2) EVEN
DISTRIBUTION =
EVEN FLOW.

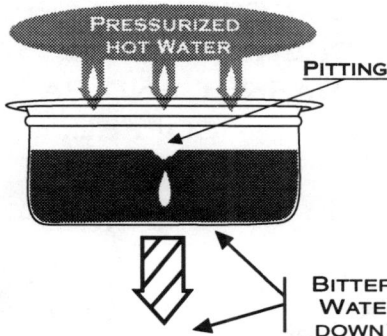

(3) PACKED SOFTLY
(LESS THAN
20 POUNDS PRESSURE).

PRESSURIZED
HOT WATER

PITTING

BITTER / THIN:
WATER GOES
DOWN THE PIT

> **BREAKING THE SEAL BETWEEN PACKED COFFEE AND BASKET WALL. PRESSURIZED WATER GOES AROUND PACKED COFFEE.**

(1) ## LOOSE GROUND COFFEE.

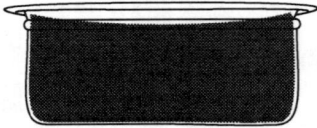

(2) ## EVENLY DOSED, DISTRIBUTED.

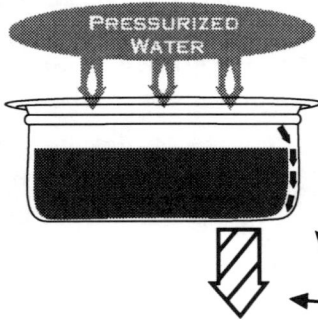

(3) ## EXCESSIVE "TAPPING" OPENS SEAL BETWEEN BASKET AND PACKED COFFEE.

PRESSURIZED WATER

BITTER / THIN EXTRACTION

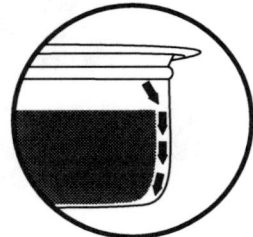

imizes opportunities for heat damage and oxidation that can occur if you grind the coffee too finely.

TAPPING

Take a look at the inset in Diagram 3. Here we see a gap between the packed coffee and the inside edge of the coffee basket.

We all tap the porta-filter during packing to dislodge loose coffee that squeezes out from under our packer and kind of creeps up the inside wall of the coffee basket. The trick is tap only once, and with just the minimum force to dislodge the coffee.

In training I have seen great baristas doing everything right except they packed and tapped, packed and tapped, many times over. This may open a gap for the brewing water to escape. The result at the spout? A cork-screwing espresso pour whitish in color with a streak of dark brown spiraling out of the porta-filter during brewing. So pack once, tap once lightly, pack again, polish with a twist of the packer and make the shot. Being quick and efficient in packing will speed up your line and keep minimize heat loss from the group-head.

The candy-stripe pour is a sure sign that pressurized brewing water is finding a path of lesser resistance in your cake of packed coffee.

(A speculative jaunt: I have often wondered why some Italian espresso machine engineers had seen fit to design espresso packers with rounded bottoms. This confused me because the coffee baskets have flat bottoms and the rounded packer created an obvious thin spot in the center of the packed coffee. Could it be that they were using the rounded shape to enhance the seal between the packed coffee and the interior wall of the basket?)

TOOLS OF THE TRADE

While visiting roasters in Northern Italy, I came across a traditional Italian flat packer. This design has been copied in part for my own packer, pictured on the following page. I have added a **slight dome** shape to the packing surface while keeping the handle the same. The slight rounding aids in particle distribution and gives us better pours than a completely flat surface.

What is not so obvious about the traditional packer, however, is that it features a stem length and handle diameter that allows continued usage with minimum strain on the human body. The small end is placed in the palm with the fingers curling around the shaft and resting against the top of the large end. This distributes forces throughout the hand for maximum control and comfort (see photograph on page 94).

The diameter of the packing end should be no more than 1 mm. smaller than the chamber that holds the ground coffee. In theory, the diameter would be exactly the same as the packed coffee chamber, but many coffee baskets are tapered, getting slightly smaller towards the bottom. If the packers are too exact, they stick in the coffee basket the first time the barista under-doses the coffee a bit.

A traditional packer is made of aluminum for lightness and balance.

TECHNIQUES OF PACKING: HOW MUCH FORCE DO YOU NEED TO PACK WITH?

Three weeks after I opened my business, my elbow started to hurt. I was packing with what I estimated to be 50 pounds of force on the packer. It was not long before I knew that Kent Bakke's example of straining to pack as hard as possible would not work in a commercial environment. I interpreted it as a training strategy to get me to understand that the espresso needs to be hard packed. Point taken, but how should we adapt this information to a daily routine?

I lightened up to about 30 pounds of force on the packer and have been happy ever since. I can make espresso coffee with 30 pounds of force on the packer for 5 hours a day, 5 days a week with no elbow or wrist problems.

Be careful not to lighten up too much, however, because weights below 20 pounds of force can result in too soft a pack and, as I have already stated, inconsistencies in the cup. (Hint: To acquaint yourself and trainees to the correct packing weight of 30 pounds of force, pack on a bathroom scale during initial training.)

After grinding, distributing, and dosing your shot, apply the packer gently at first. The first contact is mostly to ensure a level pack with even pressure.

Then withdraw the packer and tap the small end against the side of the group handle to remove coffee from the walls of the basket. Tap only once, and with just enough force to dislodge loose coffee creeping up the sides of the coffee basket. Now pack it again. (We tap with the handle end to avoid denting the business

end of the packer.) This time use 30 pounds of force, being very careful to maintain a level relationship to the rim of the porta-filter. *As you release pressure,* twist the packer around a full 360 degrees. This polishes the surface and further prepares it to be slammed with hot water at 120 pounds of force without making a pit.

The photographs on pages 89-97 show the exact grip and forearm positions of a master espresso maker. This grip is the final evolution of seven years of high volume espresso making. This grip distributes force evenly through the hand and straight up to the elbow. The wrist remains relatively straight, which is crucial.

Note that the wrist and forearm are straight up in the air. You want the force of packing to be transferred by your skeletal structure from the elbow

My Ergo-Packer is easy on the hand and features dosing lines and a slightly convex bottom for a superior pour.

through the packer in a straight line. If your forearm is not straight up and down to the direction of force, too much pressure will be placed on the wrist, which can lead to an inflammation of the tendon sheaths known as carpal tunnel syndrome.

Most members of my staff have been with me for years, hard packing the espresso for five hours a day, and most of us have had no tendon or joint problems. But if you do begin to develop aches in your wrist or elbow, learn to switch hands when you pack coffee. Pack for a week with the opposite hand to give yourself some relief.

Also, at Vivace we do not use the small end of the packer which the Italians designed to pack the single coffee shots. Italians are small cup people. Americans are big cup people. To adapt to the American market, we serve double shots, to ensure that they always get a strong caffe latte.

DRYING THE COFFEE BASKET

Before you drop the ground coffee out of the grinder into your coffee basket, dry it quickly with a cotton bar towel. This removes spent coffee, but more importantly it helps the packed coffee to adhere to the side of the coffee basket forming a watertight seal. Water likes to go where water already is. So to form a good seal, dry the basket.

COUNTERTOP HEIGHT

Some of my shorter staff members have had problems because the counters were too high for them to pack comfortably. To remedy this, we put them on a pedestal. The ideal counter height for coffee quality and comfort of staff is for the counter top to be approximately at their belt line.

PACKING AS ART

Packing is a lot like piano technique. There is a lot of hidden finesse involved in the touch and polish of a great barista.

There is a subtle smoothness in the packing motions of a great coffee maker. In watching both an accomplished barista and a new trainee, sometimes you can see very little difference in what they do with their hands. The basic mechanics look the same: grind, distribute, dose, pack and tap, pack and polish. But the coffee knows the difference. The experienced barista's shots hang like buttermilk from the spouts, so thick they appear motionless while oozing into the cup. The shots are much heavier because the barista is capturing so much of the flavor oils due to subtleties undetectable to the human eye.

So practice packing with the healthy attitude of the apprentice. It is an art of touch and finesse that comes with time and experience. A patient, respectful approach will aid in acquiring this elusive skill.

Coffee fresh from the grinder is piled unevenly
towards the front of the basket.

Begin distribution sequence drawing coffee towards you
(the 6 o'clock position) with pressure on your fingers
so it bends. The goal is to compress the ground coffee
as you pass across the top, breaking up clumps and
filling in channels.

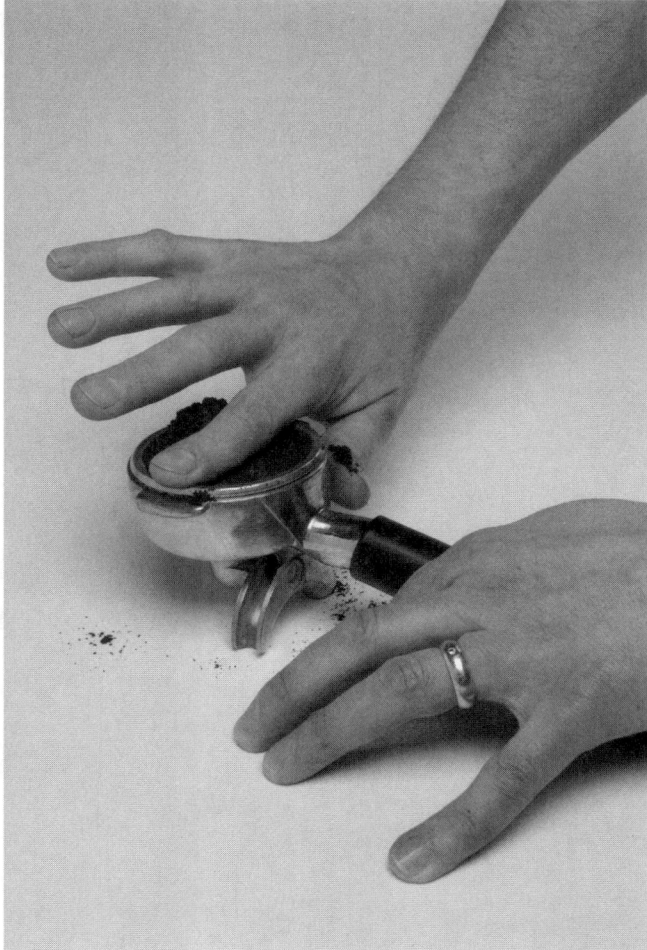

Beginning at the 6 o'clock position, compress the coffee
and move your finger towards the top of the porta-filter
(the 12 o'clock position).

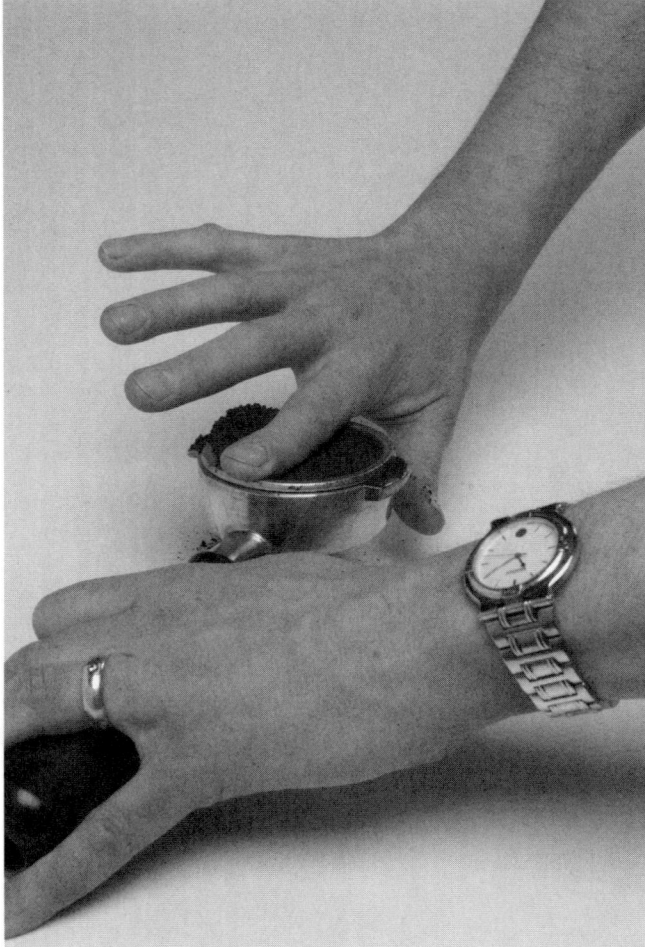

Beginning at the 3 o'clock position compress
the coffee with your finger and move it towards
the 9 o'clock position.

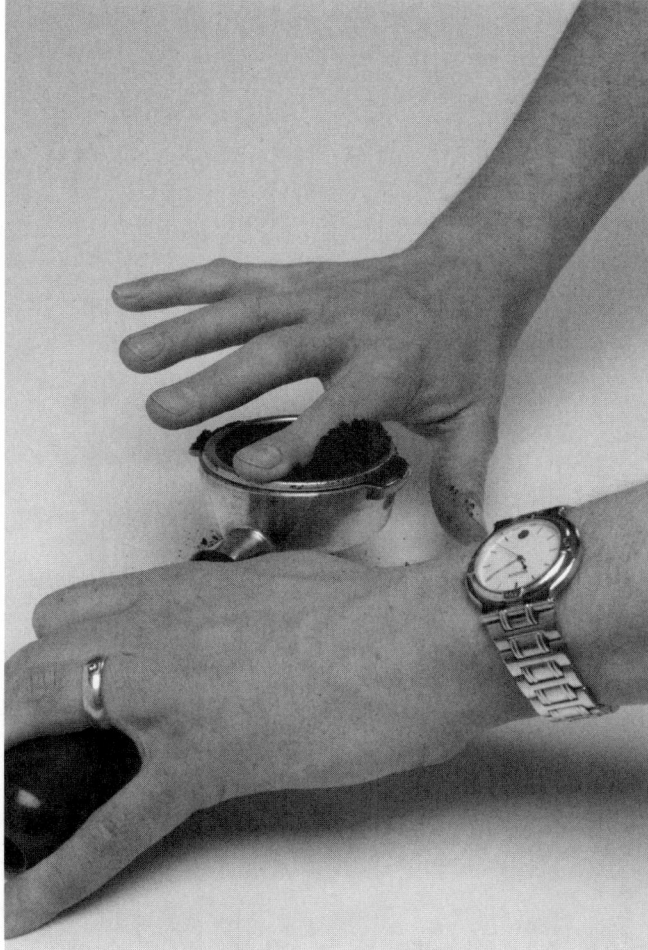

From the 9 o'clock position compress again and draw your finger back towards the 3 o'clock position. This completes distribution and coffee is ready for packing.

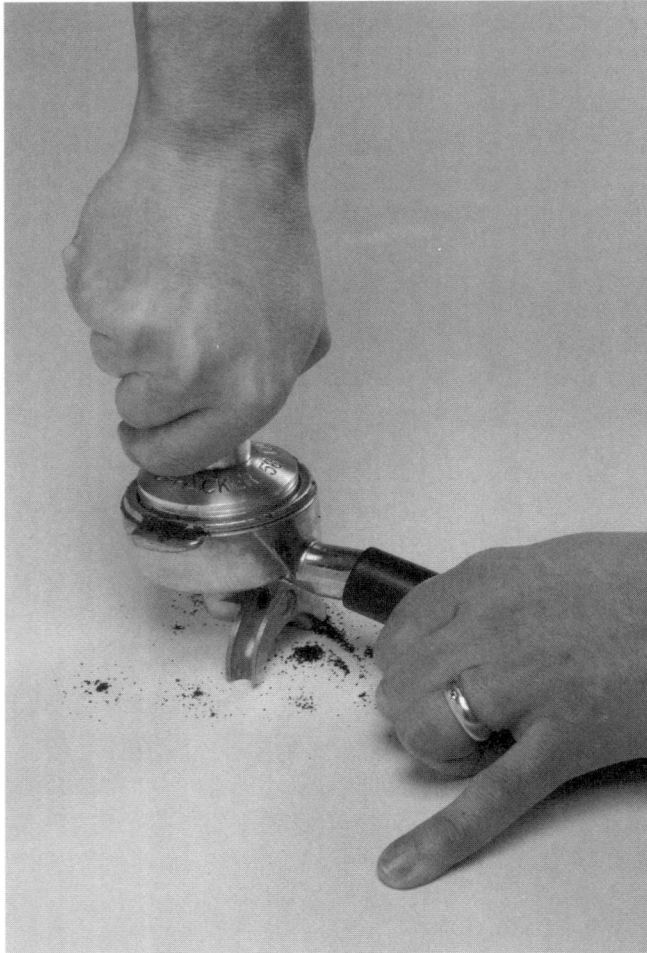

Pack straight down, concentrate on being level.
Twist packer to release it from coffee.

Tap with minimum force to dislodge coffee
from the inner wall of basket.

Pack again, straight down with 30 pounds of force.
Twist packer 720° with 5-10 pounds force applied to
"polish" the surface for even extraction.

The perfect pack. Note dosing line in coffee basket.

XIII
Espresso Dosing

Dose, the noun: An individual portion of a drug.

To dose, the verb: In the espresso process, the action of delivering ground coffee to the porta-filter and its even distribution before packing.

Keep these two definitions in mind when answering the question: How much ground coffee should be used to make the best espresso shot?

To listen to some companies, certain coffees give you more flavor by using less. The claim is usually expressed in grams used and is presumably based on the superior, stronger flavor of the coffee. This, of course, is total bunk. The truth is that there is an optimum volume for the packed espresso shot, and it is not a matter of weight.

REMEMBER, COFFEE EXPANDS

Let's first examine the word *dose* as it functions in the form of a noun. There is a way to determine how much coffee is used to make the optimum shot. It works for any machine or porta-filter/coffee basket configuration because it is based on the properties of the coffee itself, including the property of expansion during brewing.

When you are making a shot of espresso, the coffee expands, and the top of the packed cake will swell 2 to 3 mm. during the extraction process. To allow for this expansion, you must leave a space between the top of the packed coffee and the bottom of the dispersion screen.

Use this simple technique. Grind some coffee and put it into the coffee brewing basket in your porta-filter. Distribute it evenly (see photo series in *Chapter*

99

IDEAL DOSAGE OF COFFEE

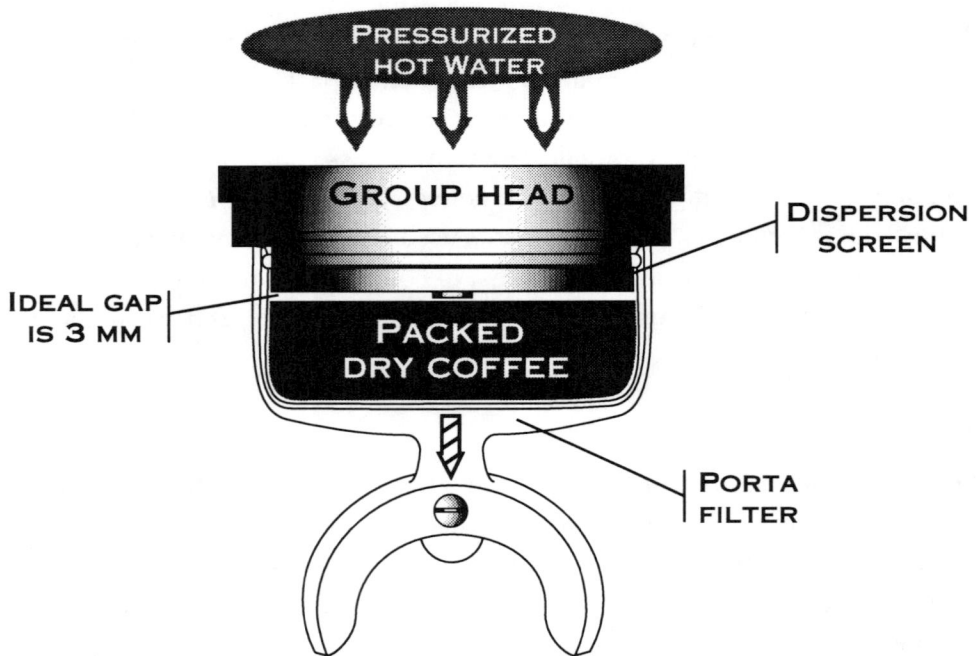

PRESSURIZED
HOT WATER

GROUP HEAD

DISPERSION
SCREEN

IDEAL GAP
IS 3 MM

PACKED
DRY COFFEE

PORTA
FILTER

UNEVEN DISTRIBUTION: WATER TAKES
THE PATH OF LEAST RESISTANCE.

1

LOOSE GROUND
COFFEE.

2

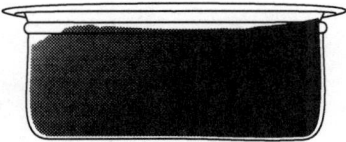

COFFEE IS <u>NOT</u>
EVENLY DISTRIBUTED.

3

PRESSURIZED
WATER

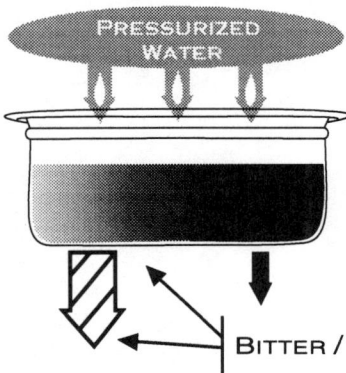

COFFEE IS
HARD PACKED.
(DENSITY IS NOT EVEN).

BITTER / THIN EXTRACTION

XII), and pack it firmly. Put the porta-filter into the machine and snug it up, just as if you were going to make a shot.

Now, instead of activating the pump, remove the porta-filter and examine the top of the packed coffee. Does it have a dent in it from the dispersion screw? Look under the group head. Is the dispersion screen caked with packed coffee?

If the coffee is mashing up against the screen or screw before brewing, the shot is overdosed. The coffee has no room for the physical expansion that occurs during brewing.

Grind some more coffee. This time when you distribute it, shave a little more off the top before packing. Repeat the above process, checking to see if the dry coffee is touching the dispersion screw or screen before brewing. Keep reducing the amount used until you have just the right packed volume to clear the bottom of the dispersal screw. It should be noted that not all machines have a protruding screw under the screen, so the key distance to remember is for the packed coffee to be about 3 mm. below the bottom of the dispersion screen. Before brewing, you should have no clumps of ground coffee on the screen.

If your shot has no room for expansion, crema texture will be adversely affected. The coffee needs a gap for brewing water to spread evenly over the surface during pre-infusion. If the ground coffee is mashed up against the screen you will have dry spots and an uneven extraction. Also, if the coffee has no room to expand, the crema will not be as heavy or feature the silkiest mouth feel, compared to a shot using the right dose. It needs a little space.

EFFECTS ON EXTRACTION RATE

Your dosage also has a big effect on the total extraction time required to make a shot. You want to extract the espresso over about a 25 second interval. Using 1 mm. more of packed coffee will slow down the extraction rate by several seconds. So, the game in dosing is to be very consistent from shot to shot. As I often state and restate, pack and dose the same every time. The only variable to change to maintain a creamy 25-second pour is the coarseness of the grind.

To achieve this consistency you will hear equipment reps from various companies tell you to grind a bunch of coffee into the dosing hopper and calibrate the dosing fins in the hopper—one click of the handle for a single or two clicks for a double.

This is a situation akin to throwing the baby out with the bath water. To achieve great espresso, each shot must be ground to order. That is why I teach people to arrange the ground coffee in a consistent pattern and volume before packing. Do it by eye, referenced to the edges of the porta-filter basket. This is actually much more accurate than the one- or two-click method and preserves all the coffees aroma and flavor for the cup.

To Dose, the Verb

As I have explained earlier in the book, water is by nature lazy and, under pressure, will take the path of least resistance. What's a poor barista to do? You must pay close attention to the distribution of the coffee before packing it, that's what.

Check out the diagrams on the next page. These are intended to depict coffee baskets cut in half to show how the coffee is packed. (Note: The coffee basket depicted is a double. We at Vivace do not use the single baskets to make espresso.)

First we see the pile of ground coffee, fresh from the grinder, appearing in the upper image before distribution. Just below that, we see it has been distributed at a very even density before packing. Then our master barista packs it with 30 pounds of pressure and a great flourishing twist to polish the surface. The result is that the pressurized water oozes through evenly. Please refer to the photographic series in *Chapter XII*.

Distribution is an essential aspect of overall technique. Not romantic or dashing to watch compared to some barista techniques, this humble activity will determine the consistency and volume of flavor you achieve. The technique is to actively pressure the coffee while measuring it. I use my index finger and press down hard enough for the finger to bow a bit and even out lumps and channels that will form as the coffee tumbles from the grinder. I employ four strokes, two at 12:00 and 6:00 if you will, and two at exactly 90 degrees to that, or 3:00 and 9:00. (Please refer to photographic sequence pgs. 89 through 97.)

Now compare this to the diagram on page 100. In the accompanying image we see the pile of loose ground coffee, but it is unevenly distributed within the coffee basket. In this case, the barista hastily shaved it off with his finger without the gentle back and forth motion to first distribute it evenly. What is the result? More ground coffee in one side of the basket before packing. If the loose coffee is

IDEALIZED EXTRACTION SERIES

(1)

LOOSE GROUND
COFFEE.

(2)

EVENLY DISTRIBUTED
AND DOSED.

(3)

PRESSURIZED
HOT WATER

HARD PACKED
& POLISHED.

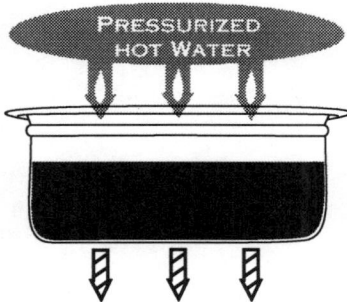

PERFECT EVEN
EXTRACTION.

not evenly arranged before packing, the packed coffee presents a path of lesser resistance for the brewing water to rush through.

In the diagram on page 100, the packed coffee of less density is over-extracted during brewing, releasing bitter flavors and caffeine. Conversely, the flavor in the portion that is of a higher density is never brought out. The small flow through that section of the packed coffee is too slow and the flavor oils that are released bum due to overexposure to hot water. The result in the cup is lousy espresso.

Rushing the distribution of loose coffee is a common mistake made even by experienced baristas when they work in a high volume espresso bar. They tend to rush. The espresso will feature a barber pole look as it comes out of the spouts, with dark streaks spiraling through a whitish, acidic-looking pour.

This aspect of water—its laziness—is omnipresent throughout the entire espresso process. Much of what the master barista is doing is designed to create an even resistance to pressurized water. Factors most affecting the resistance to water are the packing and dosing, and, of course, the grind.

XIV
Elapsed Time for a Shot

As I traveled all over Northern Italy, I was struck by the beauty of the reddish-brown espresso coffee oozing slowly from the espresso machine. From the smallest "Mom and Pop" panini bar in the mountains of the Piedmont to the famous Bar Specki in Trieste, Italian espresso always hung thickly and oozed slowly from the spouts of the espresso machine in a heavy cream. You could see that it was delicious.

As I traveled north from Milano, the espresso pours at all the places I visited became more and more watery. As I passed Lake Lugano into Switzerland, it was over. The espresso coffee gushed from the spouts in a watery brown torrent that resembled the muddy spring runoff of a mountain stream, with flavor to match.

When it comes to using an espresso machine, one of the primary errors I see is that people in a drip coffee culture seek to make a beverage that resembles drip coffee. So they use too coarse a grind and do not pack. The result? A watery, thin beverage that not only does not approach true espresso, but does not taste nearly as good as a well-made cup of drip coffee.

The first thing to remember is that an espresso machine is not related to a drip coffee system. By using pressure to foam up volatile coffee flavor oils and transport them into your cup, the espresso machine far exceeds the capabilities of drip coffee and plunger pot methods. Used properly, its unique ability to foam up soluble oils allows it to leave behind most of the bitterness and caffeine present in the ground coffee. It is a dream of efficiency—or a nightmare of bitter brew—depending largely on extraction rate.

The Italian traditions and my own research are in complete agreement. There is an ideal rate of water flow that passes through your packed, ground coffee that

will release the most soluble flavors into your espresso cup. That rate corresponds roughly to a 25-second pour. From the moment you activate the pump until all the flavor is extracted from the ground coffee, the elapsed time should be between 25 and 30 seconds. Of course, this is only true if all the other factors related to the process are in your control.

Symptoms of a pour that is too fast include thinner texture in the espresso and a lighter color. Compounds present in the whitish foam seem to attack the sweeter coffee flavors in the cup, particularly the sweet caramelized sugars of a master roast, which will be turned into an astringent bitterness. In the slightly fast pour, appearance of the crema will be thick, but will lack the dark brown flecking, called tiger mottle, that indicates perfect extraction.

If your brewing water passes too slowly through the coffee, flavor oils will burn due to over-exposure to heated brewing water. The espresso will feature black streaking on the crema and a mid-tongue bite similar in character to the taste imparted by rancid oils building up in your machine.

Perhaps the biggest difference we saw when we began using PID machines, stable to within one degree Fahrenheit, in 2001, was in the radical change in the flavor if our flow rate was off. Slow pours are still burnt, but even slightly fast pours now come out sour, as if the temperature was too low. Clearly, there is an intimate relationship between the brewing temperature and the flow rate of the espresso.

DEGREES OF SEPARATION

The espresso machine features the highest degree of separation of coffee flavor from bitter compounds and caffeine. The single factor most responsible for this separation is the extraction rate.

Take a look at the photographic series on pages 107-110, which depict an espresso pour.

In the first picture, we have activated the pump and pre-infusion begins. Remember, pre-infusion is the gentle release of brewing water onto the top of the packed coffee that occurs before pump pressure is applied. Pre-infusion creates a slight expansion of the ground coffee and acts to seal the top of the pack.

This sealing process helps to ensure that pressurized water meets an even resistance in the bed of packed coffee instead of blasting a pit in the top of the

These three degrees of roast approximate the Italian espresso-roasting spectrum.
Northern is the lightest, Central is the medium, and Southern is the darker roast.
I am certain you will find some roasters in Southern Italy going darker,
but for my tastes this is the total range of caffe espresso roasting.
Remember as the roast becomes darker, bitterness increases and acidity decreases.

The cinnamon color of the crema indicates that the
brewing water was changing temperature more than
two degrees Fahrenheit during the brewing cycle.

Brewing water temperature, held stable within a
two-degree range of error, produces the deep
red-brown crema. This color does not guarantee
that the espresso is at its best flavor potential.

The following series of photographs shows a full flavor espresso extraction with the brewing temperature stable within one degree Fahrenheit during the brewing cycle; note the color and texture.

Eight to ten seconds after the pump is activated, the elixir appears.
(Shot glasses are one ounce at the rim.)

Fifteen seconds into extraction. Note, streams are heavy—
hanging straight down from the spout.

Twenty seconds—texture is apparent.

As the color begins to become lighter we turn off the pump.
This entire cycle should take between 25 and 30 seconds.

This espresso pour has run out of flavor. The appearance of the streams coming out of the spout is whitish, and they "suck-in" due to higher surface tension. This is also the appearance of the pour with stale coffee or dull grinder burrs.

coffee where it will gush down and rob you of flavor. Pre-infusion also loosens up some flavor for easier transport to the cup.

As the pump kicks in, the pressurized water begins to soak through the packed coffee and should appear at the spouts within about 8 seconds of initiating the brewing cycle.

In the second photo, the elapsed time at this point of the cycle is about 15 seconds. The espresso is hanging at its heaviest. This is a very important stage in the pour because the first volumes of crema holds the he`aviest lipids present in the coffee and the bulk of the caramelized sugars.

As the pour progresses, the crema coming out of the spouts begins to lighten in color. This indicates the packed coffee is running out of flavor to contribute to the cup. When you notice the slightly lighter color, turn the pump off. If you turn the pump off too early, the espresso tastes heavy and cloying like a cough syrup. If the pump runs too long, the sugars in the cup perish and the espresso becomes astringent. But if it is just right, the sugars are offset with a roasty nuttiness that is balanced with varietal flavors in the aftertaste.

Experiment to determine the shot cut-off ideal for you and your roast. At Espresso Vivace the total volume for a double ristretto is 1-1/2 ounces, using 16 grams of ground coffee extracted over 25 to 30 seconds.

A Lungo vs Ristretto

At Vivace we always pour our coffee in the ristretto tradition, which means "restricted" to the most flavorful part of the shot. By keeping extraction volume small, this tradition offers the heaviest shot, thickest texture and finest flavor that the coffee has to offer.

In Italy, you may order espresso ristretto or espresso a lungo. Actual volume of a shot will vary largely with the degree of roast. Darker roasts from south of Naples feature shorter ristretto volumes, a double shot may be no more than one ounce. In the North, a doppio ristretto may approach two ounces of crema in the cup.

Espresso a lungo, literally meaning "the long pull," is thinner in texture, lacks caramelized coffee sugars and contains more caffeine than a ristretto pull. During extraction it is lighter in color coming out of the machine. This is because you

115

are diluting flavors by pushing the water through the coffee faster. Most espresso lovers, myself included, prefer espresso ristretto. Obviously, these are esthetic choices and a matter of opinion.

Of course, opinions on what tastes good can vary widely from person to person. What you need to know from me, however, is how to do the best espresso lungo if you do prefer the long pull or at least want to be able to offer it to your customers. The key is to keep the overall extraction time the same for either pouring style by adjusting the coarseness of the grind. If your lungo shot is going to be three ounces in the cup, select a slightly coarser grind setting to achieve this. The three-ounce extraction should take the same amount of time as the ristretto pour.

ADJUSTING THE EXTRACTION RATE

Throughout the day you will notice that the extraction rate of the espresso will change. Generally, as the sun comes up and humidity is removed from the air the coffee pour speeds up. As I have detailed in the section on adjusting the grind, coffee is *hygroscopic,* meaning that it readily absorbs moisture from, or releases it into, the atmosphere.

If you want to change the rate of extraction, don't alter the packing weight or the dosage. They should remain constant. Instead, if you want to slow down your extraction rate, select a slightly finer grind setting. Conversely, to speed up the pour, use a little coarser grind on the coffee.

XV
ESPRESSO SHOT VOLUME

The sad fact is that roasted coffee, with all its aromatic beauty, also contains some pretty cantankerous compounds—hostile chemical compounds, that, if allowed into your cup, will attack the lovely and fragile coffee flavors.

Fortunately for today's coffee lover, the modern espresso machine offers the highest degree of separation of these bitter flavors and coffee's flavor compounds and provides us with the most efficient coffee making process since humans first discovered the bean. But even with all of this technological support, the whole scheme is still highly dependent on human factors, such as being able to control how much brewing water is allowed to pass through the ground coffee.

Unfortunately, the single biggest mistake that I see being made the world over from Copenhagen to Seattle—is pushing too much water through the ground coffee. This is the worst possible use of an espresso machine. Not only do you miss the essence of what the espresso method should be—thick coffee that actually tastes like fresh ground coffee smells—but over-extracted espresso is much worse than a well-made cup of coffee using a drip system or plunger pot method.

THE COLOR OF FLAVOR

Whether pulling a long shot, espresso a lungo, or the connoisseur's choice, espresso ristretto, you must be diligent in cutting off the flow of water when the coffee has given you its load of flavors.

With coffee beans roasted to a deep mahogany brown, liquid coffee flavors are a rich reddish brown. You can see flavor in the espresso pour (providing that all the other factors are in your control, naturally). As you begin your espresso pour,

the flavors come out first. The trick is to coax out these precious flavors and then turn off the pump when they are exhausted.

As the flavor is transported into the cup by pressurized brewing water, it will cause the espresso crema to begin to lighten up in color as it comes out of the spout. The experienced coffee maker watches the crema, oozing into the cup, and cuts off the shot just as the color begins to lighten up. It is a matter of experience and experimentation.

In the ristretto tradition, a double dose of ground coffee, perhaps 16 grams in weight, will yield 1-1/2 ounces of pure red-brown crema. Pulling the shot this short preserves all of the coffee's most subtle and rich flavor, particularly the caramelized sugars present in the bean.

Espresso a lungo made from the same coffee should not exceed three ounces of crema in the cup. Espresso made in this fashion will lack many of the caramel tones and subtle flavors present in the short pull due to the unavoidable presence of bitter compounds that are added when shot volumes go over the two ounce mark.

These general guidelines are based on esthetic preferences. The trick for you, the espresso professional, is to taste your coffee and play with shot volumes and extraction times until you have your signature shot. What tastes the best to you?

SOME HELPFUL HINTS

1. Shot volumes are greater with a conical burr grinder. This grinding technology offers the greatest surface area of ground coffee and allows the highest extraction of flavors.

2. Espresso blends containing Central and South American coffees may be more acidic. This leads to a lemony bright flavor in the shot and shorter shot volumes due to more available acids attacking flavor compounds during extraction.

3. Dark roasts, though less acidic, contain less coffee oil within the bean. Prolonged roasting forces oils onto the surface of the coffee bean. These oils, which are the essential flavors, are exposed to the air and the harmful effects of oxidation. They quickly become rancid. Less coffee oil in the bean means less crema in the cup. Shot volumes in Naples, for example, are around one ounce for the double. Napoleon roasting traditions feature a very dark, brown bean with some visible oils on the surface, even when quite fresh.

4. Technical factors most affecting the total shot volume include loose coffee distribution during dosing, sharpness of the grinder burrs, machine cleanliness, coffee freshness, packing techniques, and brewing water temperature.

5. Due to the complexity of interrelating factors affecting total shot volumes, experienced baristas prefer semi-automatic espresso machines—machines that feature manual switching of the pump for the on and off cycles. Semi-automatic machines give the master coffee maker the most control over each and every shot made.

Of course, all automatic dosing machines can be manually switched on and off, acting as a semi-automatic, but the keypads are more expensive to replace than simple switches when they wear out.

As you become expert you will notice that all the factors affect shot volumes. The better your entire program is, the taller your shots can be before becoming lighter in color. Espresso coffee will appear to have good days and bad days. It becomes quite pixie-like in its "moods." Generally, it likes high humidity combined with low temperatures. Espresso likes foggy mornings. A good November storm makes the espresso coffee happy (and shot volumes greater) in the Pacific Northwest. Ideal, stable, brewing water temperature particularly affects shot color and volume ... and on and on and on. (Please see color photograph on page 111.)

XVI
ADJUSTING THE GRIND

Ground coffee is hygroscopic, meaning it likes to absorb or expel water molecules into the surrounding atmosphere depending on the relative humidity. This dance of the water molecules occurs very rapidly during grinding and can greatly affect pre-ground coffee sitting in the hopper.

I clearly remember getting a lesson relating to this tricky characteristic of coffee.

We had set up an espresso cart at the Fremont Fair in Seattle in the summer of 1990 and were serving constantly to a steady line of customers standing 30 people deep. Due to demand, I had let my grinder run a little longer than usual and I had half a hopper of ground coffee in the doser.

Suddenly, we felt this refreshing sea breeze sweep off the ship canal. All the parched customers waiting in the beating sunlight enjoyed the relief of the cool maritime air, but my coffee stopped dead. I had the grind set to a perfect 25-second pour. It was buttery looking and perfect. I set the next shot into the machine, the same as the one I had pulled 10 seconds prior, turned on the pump and ... nothing. Not a drop came out of the porta-filter.

I had to dump out the ground coffee because it had absorbed so much moisture, so quickly, that it acted as if the grind was much too fine. Extraction rates slow down as humidity increases, because the moisture allows the ground coffee to be more adhesive. This adhesive quality results in a greater resistance to the flow of pressurized water.

In about 20 seconds, I was forced to loosen my grind by eight small divisions ("ticks" in our parlance), to recapture my 25 second extraction rate (adjustment made on a Mazzer Normale grinder). This remains the single largest grind change I have ever witnessed in eight years of professional espresso work.

WHAT IS THE POINT OF THIS TALE?

The point of the story is that to make espresso at its finest, there is no other system except to grind for each cup individually. By doing this, not only do you protect all the coffee's volatile flavors from oxidation, but you have the finest degree of control over changing atmospheric conditions.

This is the essence of our method—to make tiny, almost continuous adjustments in the grind as the day progresses and conditions, mostly humidity, change. Grinding by the cup is the only way to stay close to the all-important extraction time of 25 seconds (please see *Chapter XIV: Elapsed Time for the Shot* for details).

As I have stressed repeatedly, the grind is the only adjustment a professional barista should make to keep the extraction rate consistent. Hold the dosage and the packing weight constant.

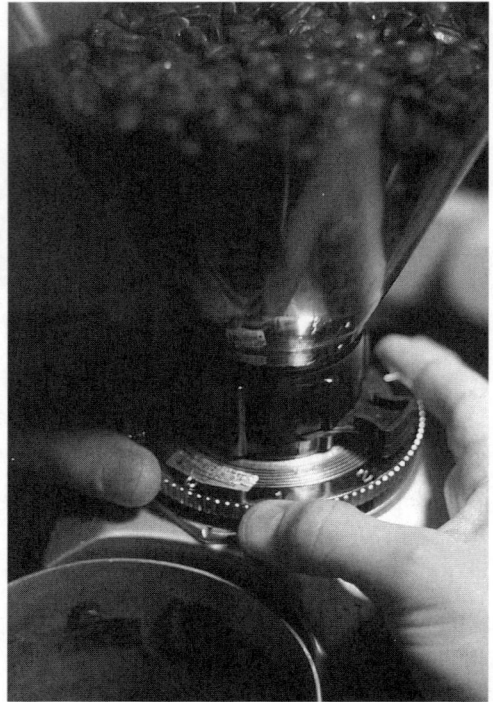

To maintain a perfect rate of extraction, the only adjustment a barista makes is changing the coarseness of the grind. Hold packing weight and dosage constant.

THE TECHNIQUE

When a customer orders, we switch on the grinder and grind just enough for the shot. We dose, distribute and pack the coffee, then fire off the shot. We follow this same procedure for each order.

We watch the coffee. If it comes out too quickly, under 25 seconds for our 1-1/2 ounce double, we make a small adjustment in the grind to make it a touch finer. Then we try again. If it comes out too slowly, sort of drip-dripping along with no real thickness and taking longer than 30 seconds to achieve our target volume, we will make the grind a little coarser. All the while, we hold dosage and packing weight as near to constant as possible.

With practice, a professional espresso maker knows if the grind is off simply with a glance at the pour. Perfect espresso looks thick and heavy as it oozes out of the machine.

Usually the changes in humidity are gradual and small adjustments are made constantly. It is perfectly analogous to a violinist playing outdoors. The wood of the instrument expands and contracts slightly with changes in temperature, altering the pitch. The violinist makes tiny tuning adjustments to compensate. The Fremont Fair story was a drastic situation, not at all the norm in day-to-day espresso making.

TRICKS AND TRAPS

The Seasoning Shot

As I have mentioned in *Chapter VII: Machine Cleanliness,* after cleaning the group handles you must make a seasoning shot. It is like the sauce chef seasoning a pan that has been scoured clean before he can create the great sauce. Well, for reasons I do not yet fathom, the seasoning shot comes out about 5 seconds quicker than the shot following seasoning. Do not adjust your grind based on a seasoning shot. Instead, make another shot to see how your coffee is behaving.

Popcorning, the Amy Effect

One of my all-time best coffee makers, Amy Vanderbeck, noticed that if you empty the bean hopper of beans during the process of grinding a shot, that particular shot will come out too fast. When the beans get too low in the bean hopper, the beans bounce around (like popcorn) entering the burrs. This leads to an inconsistent grind.

Leftover Ground Coffee

This one is a bit devilish. No one wants to throw coffee away. Yet, working in a high volume environment, it is very difficult to grind exactly the amount you need each time someone places an order. Most baristas end up scraping some coffee back into the hopper during the dosing/distribution sequence. As harmless as this practice might seem, the reality is that even a little bit of leftover coffee will rapidly absorb or expel water molecules. This trapped coffee will have a very different extraction rate than the freshly ground coffee it mixes with for the next order.

The only solution to this problem is precision work. The more accurate the barista is at grinding the right amount for each shot and evenly distributing the coffee, the better his or her coffee will be.

Hidden Ground Coffee

Some grinders, including the conical burr DRM machine, have a chamber that the ground coffee passes through on the way to the dosing hopper. This chamber may trap up to 10 grams of ground coffee. This trapped coffee means that if you adjust the grind, the new grind will not take full effect until the chambered coffee is used up.

Sounds like no problem, eh?

Well, what if it is a warm day or your grinder has been very active and is heating up (see *Chapter IV: The Espresso Grinder*) and that ground coffee sits there for 2 or 3 minutes before you make a shot? This can strip away moisture and flavor from the trapped coffee, resulting in a very fast pour when the barista uses it.

Then what do you do? You may make a big grinder adjustment. Let's see, David said if it's too fast, make the grind finer. What happens next? Nothing comes out of the machine at all. The mistake is that you made a big grind adjustment based on the rate of extraction presented by the trapped, desiccated coffee. We call this being "lost in the noise."

What you need to do if the grinder is going to sit idle for a minute or two is clean out the aperture with a grinder brush. Grinder brushes look like round paint brushes and should be available from your equipment representatives.

XVII
CLEANING TECHNIQUES
KEEPING THE ESPRESSO MACHINE SWEET WHILE YOU WORK.

Coffee flavors are volatile, sensitive compounds that can be adversely affected by any number of factors. Nowhere is this more apparent than in relationship to machine cleaning. Espresso coffee that has been prepared on a dirty espresso machine attacks the taste buds with a mid-tongue bite that registers as a bitter-sour flavor. In fact, a clean espresso machine will foul in about 40 minutes after making a shot of espresso if oily deposits in the porta-filter and within the group head are left to become rancid.

CLEANING TECHNIQUES

Clean your machine while working with the following techniques:

Scrubbing

While we are open and serving espresso coffee, we pop out the coffee baskets every 45 minutes or so and scrub out the oily deposits in the porta-filter using a Scotch Brite® pad. This is accomplished in about 15 seconds. (Note: Cut pads into two-inch squares and keep a few on top of the machine. A square will scrub about five porta-filters before it is worn out.)

Best results are obtained by rinsing the exposed porta-filter under the hot water jet from the large steam boiler. This water, which is about 205 degrees Fahrenheit, will strip out excess oils while adding heat to the metal itself. Then quickly, but vigorously, scrub out the interior and the spout beneath before the porta-filter has a chance to cool off.

Rinse again under the hot water jet, then pop the coffee basket back in and restore the porta-filter to the group head. The game is to be thorough, but quick. Do not let the porta-filter cool off while working the bar.

We leave the spent coffee puck in the basket at all times while working because the machines seem to make better coffee if the old coffee puck is left in the porta-filter until the next shot is made. I speculate that the heat trapped in the wet coffee grounds helps prevent the porta-filter from cooling off. I must admit I am not sure why the next shot comes out sweeter if the spent coffee remains in the coffee basket, but it does in our experience.

Scrubbing needs to be done every 45 minutes, regardless of volume of coffee served. Espresso machines are designed for continuous service. Oils in the group head and porta-filter become rancid less quickly when making espresso continuously.

Stewing

If after reading this you get all excited and run to your espresso machine, pop out the coffee baskets only to find a black, baked-on mass of rancid coffee deposits, I have a little trick for you. We call it stewing.

Take a one liter steam pitcher and fill it half way with hot water. Add one tablespoon of Tri Sodium Phosphate (TSP)* to the water and insert your dirty porta-filter, without the coffee basket in it. Now heat the solution just to a boil with your steamer. When the solution comes to a boil, it strips out all coffee deposits instantly.

This is a neat timesaving trick. However, check with your local health department on proper rinsing procedures after stewing your porta-filters.

---

*Tri sodium phosphate is a versatile cleaning product and is the active ingredient in espresso detergents. However, espresso detergents have some agents in them to prevent the TSP from attacking rubber gaskets and valves in your espresso machine. Never substitute TSP for espresso detergent when back flushing your machine.

Rinsing the Heads

Each time you make a shot of espresso, your backflush valve releases pressure inside the group head to prevent hot pressurized coffee filth from shooting all over the place when you remove the porta-filter. So the obvious question is: Where does all the liquid coffee sludge go? Most of it goes down a special drain network, which shares a tube and valve with your brewing water delivery system inside your espresso machine. But some oily crud remains in the group head unless you flush it out. This black water will foul your next shot of espresso and your machine unless you get rid of it each time you make an espresso coffee.

At minimum, you must remove the porta-filter and quickly release about an ounce of water through the head, then replace the porta-filter in the head again. Now you are ready to make another shot. (Try this simple test: Make a shot. When you are finished, remove the porta-filter and run two ounces of water from the head into a white ceramic cup. Check it out. Do you want this stuff sitting in your machine or going into your customer's cup?)

Clearwater Backflushing

Keep a porta-filter on top of the machine that is fitted with a blind filter (the "coffee basket" with no holes in it). This is your backflush handle.

After dumping out the dirty water, backflush once or twice to forcefully flush out any remaining pollutants. Remember, to backflush, activate the pump against the blind filter until it is fully pressurized, then release the pressure. If done correctly, you should hear the flushing sound behind the head.

When you remove the blind filter, examine the water found in it. Are there little chunks of coffee in it? If so, you may be overdosing the coffee and it is crushing against the dispersion screens during extraction (see *Chapter XIII: Espresso Dosing*).

It is also possible to have coffee grounds on your group head gasket. To rinse this off, use your blind filter again but do not tighten it all the way into the group head. Activate the brewing pump and allow a little water to overflow around the edges of the blind filter. This will rinse off the group gasket. It helps to wiggle the porta-filter handle a bit while the hot water flows over the top of the blind filter.

Remember! When rinsing at the head of the machine do not run more than

two ounces of water through at a time. You can drive your machine below your target temperature if you run excess water through the group head.

Backflushing with Espresso Detergent

Backflushing with detergent while serving is a bit tricky. Espresso detergent is difficult to rinse out of the group head and tastes awful if it gets into your coffee. To clean with detergent while serving, rinsing out the detergent is the critical phase.

If you find that a dirty machine taste is creeping into your espresso during serving hours, despite scrubbing and backflushing the heads, follow these rinsing guidelines in order to keep detergent out of the coffee after cleaning. (At Vivace, we clean the machines after every four hours of operation.)

Review the cleaning procedures for the machine and detergent you are using. We use 1-1/4 teaspoons of detergent on a 30-second wash cycle. Release pressure after 30 seconds and backflush at least two more times while the detergent remains in the blind filter. Remove the porta-filter and activate the pump to rinse out the detergent within the head.

The most effective technique I know of to clear the detergent out of the head is to rock the brewing switch on and off at one-second intervals. This pushes the soapy water out of the dispersion screen and back out the backflush drain. Repeat this procedure until water looks clear coming out of the head.

Then backflush at least five times. Rinse the blind filter at a sink or under the steam boiler water jet until totally *free* of detergent. Replace the blind filter into the head and backflush a minimum of five times. Visually examine, smell, and feel the water in the blind filter, searching for any traces of detergent. Repeat rinsing as necessary.

Seasoning

Just as a master chef must season a sauce pan prior to cooking, your group head and porta-filter must receive a fresh coat of coffee oils after cleaning and before preparing gourmet espresso. Without the benefit of a seasoning shot, the bare metal will impart a sharpness to the first shot of coffee out of the machine.

Another concern with cleaning while serving is that running all this water

through the heads can drive your machine several degrees under your target temperature. If the temperature is down, the first few shots may be a cinnamon color with no tiger mottle in the crema—and feature a disagreeable sour taste.

Anyway you look at it, cleaning with detergent will disrupt your program for a few minutes under the best of circumstances. Let your taste buds guide you in your decision to clean or not to clean.

High Volume Technique

When continuously making shots, you may not need as much clearwater backflushing. After each shot just remember to dump the dirty water, two ounces, out of the head just after you make a shot of coffee.

Your scrubbing schedule will be the same. Scrub your porta-filters every 45 minutes.

Slow Bar Technique

Keeping the espresso sweet when making a shot every ten minutes or so is quite difficult. You face two problems: the porta-filters cool off too much and accumulated oils seem to go rancid more quickly. To combat this problem, as a customer places an order, activate the pump and run two ounces of water through the head and porta-filter to heat it up a bit. (This preheating will also trap some dirty coffee oils in the head, so run an ounce of water through the head before making the next shot.)

When the customer is served, rinse the dirty water out, and backflush the group if you do not expect to make another shot right away. (Excess backflushing can cool the machine. It may be wise to pre-heat the blind-filter with water from the steam boiler before backflushing.)

The clearwater backflushing step is essential in a slow bar situation.

CLOSING PROCEDURES

After you are finished serving, always clean your machine thoroughly.

Remove the dispersion screens and scrub the heads of the machine with your Scotch Brite® pads. Run your gasket brush around each head gasket. Backflush with espresso detergent. Then replace the screens.

Scrub out porta-filters and soak overnight in a solution of TSP or espresso detergent dissolved in water. Do not submerge the plastic handles because the cleaners will erode the plastic.

Remove steamer tips and clean out the holes with a pin. Wipe wands clean and restore the tips. Do not soak them overnight because a power failure will create a suction and draw the scummy soaking solution into the boilers.

Of course, remove drain trays and cup racks and rinse clean.

This is the time to polish your machine. The machines like this and will break down less often. And they will view you, their human, as an okay appendage.

XVIII
MILK TEXTURING & PRESENTATION

THE TEXTURE

With an artistic touch, a steamer wand can literally perform magic. In the right hands, milk can be transformed into a thick chiffon that has the feel of the finest satin on the tongue. This ultra-fine foam varies in density from very hard (with minimum air injected into the milk) for pouring the Rosetta Latte, to a soft density for the espresso conjurer's greatest feat—Cappuccino.

How dense the foam becomes all depends on how you steam the milk. To put it all into perspective, I am reminded of the Eskimo traditions of having many words for the different forms of snow. The same can be said for making espresso, where we have latte texture, macchiato texture and cappuccino texture.

Ultra-fine texture is the only desirable foam consistency for espresso making. My argument is that there is no other foam because the texture not only offers the most velvet-like mouth feel, but it also enhances to the highest degree coffee's flavor. Beautiful milk art patterns are only possible with the dense, micro-bubble foam as well.

Big bubble foam (we call it sea foam, being from the coastal lands of the northwestern United States) is not only ugly to see, but the large air bubbles prevent coffee flavor from saturating your taste buds. It is simple really: where there is an air bubble on your tongue, there is no espresso.

So here I abandon my careful facade of objectivity. All pretense of being open to other styles of espresso making is abandoned, and I hereby take a firm stance on milk texture. Whatever your style of espresso there is only one truth: milk texturing featuring ultra-fine bubbles will enhance your coffee's flavor, mouth-feel and appearance. It is the only choice to perfect the cuisine.

The Technique

I like to tell my students that milk texturing has a steep learning curve, but is a relatively small hill. On the other hand, espresso making seems easy at first, with a gentle learning curve, but you are ascending a vast mountain. With milk texturing you can master the creation of the foam in one day if you know the techniques. In espresso extraction, the more you discover, the less you know.

Please refer to the diagrams on the following page. In Diagram 1 is a pitcher, 2/3 of a liter in capacity, with fresh, cold milk filling it up about half way. The tip of the steamer is positioned so that the holes for the steam are 1/2 inch or so beneath the surface of the milk. Then we apply full steam.

Presentation enhances the appeal of espresso coffee.

STEAMING THE MILK

1

STEAMER TIP
NEAR TOP OF
MILK FOR
"STRETCHING".

(45° - 100°F)

2

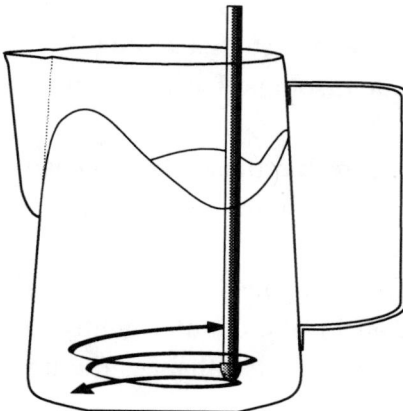

STEAMER TIP
IS LOWERED TO
CAUSE MILK TO
WHIRLPOOL.

(100° - 150°F)

As the milk heats, we remain motionless, perhaps lowering the pitcher a millimeter or two. It is done by ear. We are listening for the slight hissing that indicates that some air is being drawn into the milk. The milk rises quickly, expanding with air. If it splatters all over, the steamer tip is too high, so raise the pitcher a little bit. If you do not hear any hissing sounds, lower the pitcher a tiny bit. The hissing is air being drawn into the milk. Drawing air into the milk should only be done when the milk is cool to the touch, below 100 degrees. Drawing air into the milk above 100 degrees will create larger bubbles in the foam.

In Diagram 2, the milk volume has expanded to fill 2/3 of the pitcher just as the temperature has reached 100 degrees Fahrenheit (an elapsed time of perhaps 5 seconds; of course, heating times vary a bit with machine size. My data is gathered using a Marzocco 3-Group Linea).

We can introduce air by placing the steamer very close to the surface, *but only when the milk is cool to the touch—that* is, the milk is below 100 degrees. As we pass through 100 degrees, this completes the stretching phase of milk texturing.

Notice that we have submerged the steamer and moved it from center to the right side of the pitcher. This begins the all-important whirlpool phase of milk texturing.

Above 100 degrees it is crucial to establish a spinning volume of milk (usually clockwise works best for some reason) to whip the air into the micro-bubble lattice. If you break the surface with the steam when the milk is above 100 degrees you will introduce large bubbles, grain we call it, and it will be difficult to obtain the perfect texture.

When the milk reaches 150 degrees or so, we stop steaming. We are careful to be fluid and precise in our motions while turning off steam, avoiding bringing the steamer to the surface at all costs.

After steaming, combine the milk with fresh espresso as soon as possible. If you are waiting for the shot to be done, keep spinning the milk manually by whirling the pitcher.

If you have any undesirable big bubbles riding the top of the milk after steaming (we call this "lace"), pound the pitcher on the counter gently, and whirl it forcefully. Whirling after steaming is a great trick, it enhances the finest texture while acting to thicken the silky foam.

A tricky point in the cuisine is that resteamed milk is not as sweet and will not texture well, as compared to fresh milk. But no one likes to waste milk. It becomes a game of efficiency. Can you steam just the right amount for the order? Yes, if you are serving a caffe latte at 12 ounces, but it is not possible when serving cappuccino at 7 ounces. You need a certain volume to achieve texture. (I use only the .6 liter pitcher unless steaming for two tall lattes at once). You will need to play with this concept a lot to fine-tune your program.

When combining fresh milk with residual milk left over from the last order, follow the rule. You can stretch if the mixture of milk is cool. If the milk is warm before you steam it be careful to spin it with steam power. That is submerge the steamer tip, and do not break the surface of the milk with the steam jet.

Machine Setup

Great foam is not possible if there is too much water in your steam boiler. It comes out with the surface looking like slug trails, sort of shiny and slimy. The reason for this is that the steam is too wet.

Set your boiler water level at just above half way in your sight glass. Machines vary, so check with your equipment representative on how to vary the ratio between hot water and steam space within the boiler. (Most machines use a probe that is sticking out of the top of the steam boiler with a little white Teflon sleeve to insulate it. This probe is gently raised to raise the water level and lowered to lower the water level. The tip of the probe determines the top of the water level. Never go below half way in your boiler sight glass, because you may expose the heat exchanger within the boiler if you have a heat exchange type of machine. And of course, never adjust your machine with the power on. See the photograph on page 39 in *Chapter V: The Espresso Machine.*)

Steamer Tip

You need a four hole steamer tip, at minimum, with a fanlike dispersion pattern. See the diagram on the next page.

PITCHER SIZE AND SHAPE

It may be due to familiarity, but I get the best milk texture from the straight-walled pitcher with tapered sides and a pouring spout. The rosetta latte is particularly dependent on the pouring spout.

Pitchers shown here are one liter, $2/3$ of a liter and the smallest is about $1/3$ of a liter (see photograph on next page).

THE STEAM WAND

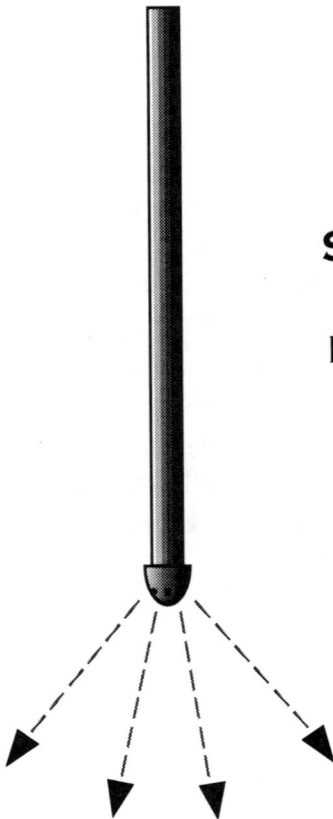

STEAM EXITS WAND IN A FAN PATTERN FROM <u>FOUR</u> HOLED STEAMER TIP.

On a commercial three group machine, steam pressure is suitable to drive a larger pitcher of milk to achieve the whirlpool. The smallest pitcher size you can use on this machine is really the 2/3 liter. In my Roasteria, we use a 2/3 liter pitcher for every drink we prepare unless we have two tall lattes on the bar in one order. Then we use the one liter.

The key is to match steamer power to pitcher size. If the steam is too powerful, the milk can be blown out over the rim of the pitcher during the whirlpool phase of steaming. With finesse, partial steam pressure can be applied to offset this problem.

If the steamer is not powerful enough, the milk will not spin properly. This is crucial. If you can not achieve the whirlpool, you can not texture the milk.

The Milk

Whole milk is 4% milk fat in Washington State. Perfect texture is possible for all milk varieties, with nonfat being the most difficult.

Pitchers feature straight, tapered walls and pouring spouts. from left to right: one liter, .6 liter and .36 liter.

Nonfat milk requires almost no stretching phase. It fluffs up easily and will turn into big bubble "sea foam" with the slightest injection of too much air. Also, nonfat will separate most quickly in the pitcher into dry foam on top with runny hot milk underneath. Nonfat must be served immediately after steaming. Not even the trick of whirling the pitcher will save your nonfat milk if your espresso shot is delayed.

In general, the more milk fat the milk contains the more aggressively it needs to be stretched during the initial phase of steaming. Follow this rule and get to know the various milks in your neighborhood.

Perfect texture results in a mirror-like finish on the surface of steamed milk.

MILK TEXTURE FOR THE CLASSICAL ESPRESSO MENU

Cappuccino

In Northern Italy, cappuccino is steamed milk and espresso coffee served in a six- or seven-ounce cup. It is traditionally enjoyed in the morning with a roll called brioche (the Italian breakfast). It is not uncommon for Italians to order cappuccino without foam. The defining aspect of cappuccino is not the texture but the ratio of espresso to milk, about 5 parts to one and served in a bowl-shaped porcelain cup of no more than 7 ounces total capacity.

That being said, the marvel of a well-made cappuccino is the silky milk texture combined with a sweet espresso coffee. However thick you make the foam, there should be no visible bubbles, and the thick milk should blend evenly with the espresso as it is poured.

For cappuccino, start with an empty 2/3 liter pitcher. Add fresh, *cold* milk up to the base of the spout, about half way up the height of the pitcher. Steam it, carefully avoiding big bubbles but at the same time expanding it to 3/4 of the pitcher's volume. When finished, you have a thick texture with no visible bubbles. Now, to achieve the ultimate density and mouth feel, spin the milk by whirling the pitcher aggressively for at least 30 seconds, preferably while the shot is coming out of the machine.

If you have done it correctly, the top of the milk will become like glass, so reflective that it looks like white chrome, but it is still pourable. Now combine the milk with the espresso in a seven-ounce porcelain cup using a gentle shaking motion of the pitcher. The gentle shaking will pour off the thickest foam from the top of the steamed milk. Serve with a spoon.

Espresso Macchiato

Espresso macchiato means espresso marked with a bit of milk and is usually enjoyed in the mid-morning with a stirring of sugar. At Vivace, we prefer to steam the milk for a thick texture, not unlike cappuccino. Steam in your smallest pitcher. Serve in the small cup, or tazzina, and always with a spoon on the side.

The Porcelain Cups: Tazza and Tazzina

Espresso is not usually served in paper cups in Northern Italy. You do not see

Italians whizzing about, clutching poly-lined or styrofoam cups. The coffee is enjoyed in the bar and served in thick-walled porcelain cups.

Espresso is a fleeting, delicate little dab of red-brown crema. It is a unique combination of flavor and texture, with qualities that are changing from the instant it is served. Texture collapses quickly as the heavy foam, called crema, dissipates. The crema holds the most delicate aromatic flavors of the coffee, suspended in the microscopic lattice of air and lipids. If it sits around, these flavors are released into the atmosphere. For this reason, Italians always enjoy their coffee in the bar.

The traditional tazzina is a small cup that has evolved to enhance and preserve the crema of espresso ristretto. It features a thick porcelain wall and is preheated by the barista before espresso is drawn into it. The porcelain composition retains heat and cradles the little dollop of pure coffee flavor for the few moments before it is sugared, then savored.

The tazza is a wide-mouth, bowl-shaped cup of no more than 7 ounces total volume. It has a handle. It also is made of thick-walled porcelain and is preheated on top of the machine to preserve espresso crema. It has a wide top to display the lovely swirling patterns of a master coffee maker.

Espresso is always drawn into the same cup in which the customer is to be served. Cups are always stored on top of the machine in the special cup trays that are designed to heat them gently from the boilers below. Tazza are always heated again with hot water before espresso coffee is prepared.

Milk Art Patterns: Espresso as a Culinary Art

Pouring a beautiful heart or rosetta on your caffe latte or cappuccino is the mark of the gourmet in espresso preparation. Why do I say this? It is because its mastery is only achieved for the personal pleasure of the coffee maker. If you thrill to the beauty of the espresso, the patterns will be yours with time.

It is even more true of the espresso. If the passion is not present in your heart for things you eat and drink, you will never master gourmet espresso. It is just too tricky of a cuisine. If you are going into this business because it is the "hot trend" right now, you go to your own slaughter. And, you deserve your fate. The motivations of getting rich quick or aggressive national expansion dreams will always lead you away from the essence of the coffee, which is beauty.

Forgive my cheeky posturing, but the passion and love required to perfect the espresso are also its golden promise. If you master the coffee and create a loyal following that appreciates the coffee you make, you will be in business for life. Neither technical innovation nor big-budget marketing can ever capture the imagination of your loyal customers as much as your own personal desire to achieve the perfect espresso coffee. It is the ideal form for a small business: creating beauty and making people happy for a moment in return for a fair living standard. In the espresso business, there will never be a "category killer" forcing you out of business.

My warning is to stay with the coffee, stay small. Sit right on your cuisine like a fine gourmet chef, which is what you are. Avoid the siren song of franchising, do not go into heavy marketing or spend all your time trying to open too many shops. The coffee will leave you if you leave it, and the customers will soon be gone too.

The following four photographs demonstrate pouring the rosetta latte.

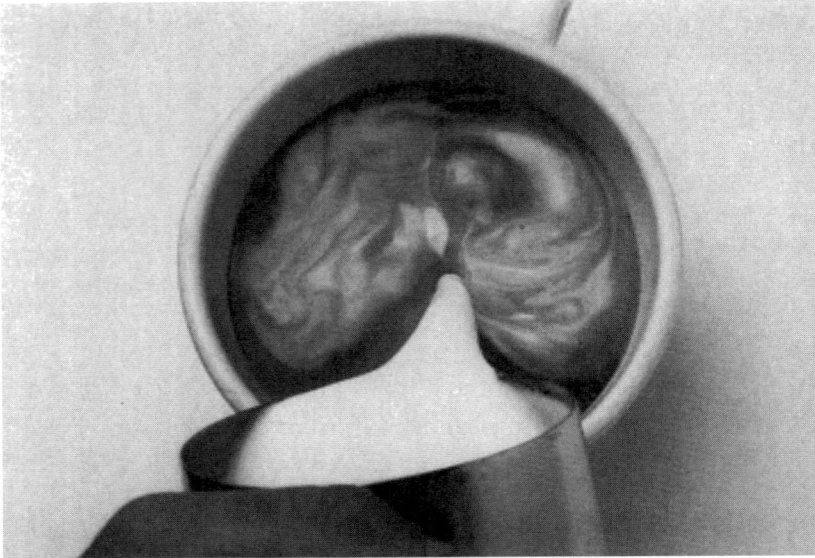

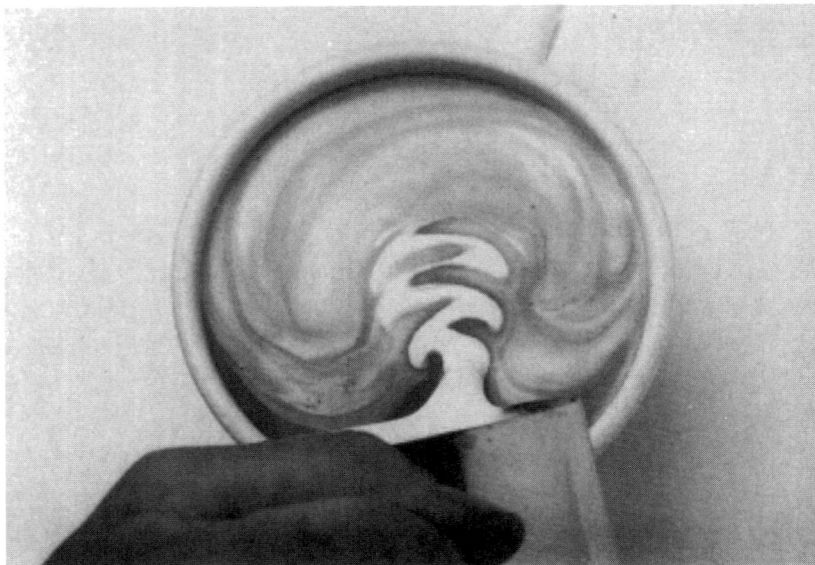

Begin shaking and "backing up" the pitcher as you near the top of the cup.

Now reverse the direction of the pitcher and pour through the center of the "flower petals."

Voila!

XIX
STAFF TRAINING
CREATING A CULTURE OF EXCELLENCE

In my travels documenting espresso coffee, I have encountered several individuals in the business who at least tried to make fine espresso coffee. But I have never seen anyone create a staff that was just as excited about coffee as they were. The old truth about running a business holds especially true for an espresso bar: Nothing is as difficult as hiring, training, and motivating a staff.

HIRING

How do we hire good people for manning the espresso machine? And, what do we teach them when we take them on?

The first point to consider is that the coffee business is a customer service business. In my opinion, customer service people are born, not made. You need an alert, observant person who possesses an easy confidence with people and a tolerably clean appearance. In short, you need a people person. The best you can do is to refine these innate essential qualities, but some people are simply not customer service types.

In hiring a potential espresso specialist, one of the key qualities to look for is a person who displays a certain pickiness with their coffee. The best baristas are very fussy about their craft. They want it just so. To start an interview, I may make a candidate a perfect cappuccino. Do their eyes light up upon tasting it? No lights may mean no barista. Are they excited about food, wine, beer? Any sign that an applicant is connected to their taste buds is a good sign. Some kind of culinary interest and excitement *must* be present.

For work experience I prefer a background in bartending.

At Vivace we always hire with a team. My trusted managers and business partner must all approve a candidate before we will take him or her on.

As a high volume business we have enough work to create an entry level position, a barback. This is a tough job which requires performing tasks such as running errands, stocking and cleaning ashtrays, for little pay. The person who can handle the barback position shows a strong sense of priorities and a strong work ethic. If we like the performance as barback, and we see he or she is excited about the coffee, he or she is slotted for a barista position.

TRAINING

Training is an ongoing process and should not be viewed as a one-time event that a new employee undertakes. Any in-depth training takes place within the context of a "company culture." Each organization will form its own way of doing things based on staff perceptions of the priorities of the owners. Thus, the priorities of the owners will either erode training goals or reinforce them.

For example, if a stated training goal for your espresso pour is a 25-second extraction, that statement should be reinforced by providing easy-to-read timing devices during the training period. Instead of just stating goals, owners and managers need to show commitment. You must carefully analyze your own priorities in order to earn the respect of your employees toward your training goals. That being said, what do we teach them, and, more importantly, how do we make it stick?

Employees expected to make espresso should be given at least a week of intensive training on the fundamentals of espresso preparation. Anyone attempting to specialize in the making of espresso coffee needs to control each variable in order to approach perfection. Some variables on the list are in the realm of specialists, such as in-depth machine maintenance and repair.

I personally teach the theory stuff first. I explain and draw pictures to show how coffee volatility and the properties of pressurized water affect the espresso process (see *Chapter II: Espresso Theory*). Sit them down and give them context by which they can understand technique. If you take the time to establish this context, your technical training will be retained longer by the trainee.

After a 20-minute theory discussion, we go to the machines. I break down shot making for the trainee into the following categories:

1. Dosing, distribution and packing. We do this until they get it. Grinding a shot, evenly distributing it, then dosing and packing it perfectly over and over until they have it in their minds and in their hands. It may take five minutes or an hour, depending greatly on the physical talents of the trainee.

2. Adjusting the grind for a 25-second pour. I show them how to adjust the grind, holding packing weight and dosage constant, to change the rate of water flow through the packed coffee.

3. Cleaning techniques are covered next. Scrubbing the porta-filter approximately every 45 minutes, rinsing dirty water from the heads after each shot you make, and backflushing between groups of customers. We also cover cleaning with espresso detergent during this phase of training.

4. Thermal Control—Temperature Surfing. I teach them to be quick, not allowing the porta-filter to cool off while packing, and manipulating the temperature of the head with 2-ounce pulses of brewing water to achieve a target temperature.

This is the content of my initial training program and can be accomplished with most students within four hours. It is important to note that my best baristas are never my quickest students at first. This probably is just a statistical anomaly, but intriguing just the same. Maybe the ones who respect the coffee are cautious and fumbly at first.

I never teach milk to a new trainee, and all my baristas work in teams. A new barista works the shot making side of the machine, while the other steams milk and runs the cash register and supervises the newcomer's coffee for a few weeks. When I see that they are getting a feel for the coffee, we go into milk, details of the cuisine, etc. It usually takes about 4 weeks for a barista to be allowed to solo on a bar while his or her partner takes a break or does dishes.

In my first two years of business, before my company culture formed, training was much slower. Now information is reinforced from all sides as the newcomer makes his or her way into the staff. Also, there is a healthy attitude of competition among staff to excel.

The Macchinesti

For a business to be successful at producing high quality espresso coffee, an individual must be appointed as quality control technician for the operation. In Italian culture this person is called the macchinesti, the espresso machine specialist.

He or she needs to be in direct contact with staff and the coffee each barista makes on a daily basis. This person must adjust the machines, change dull grinder burrs, taste and praise good results and correct bad habits before they work their way into the company culture.

In my opinion, the best form of the espresso business is when the macchinesti is the owner. If the coffee passion and knowledge reside in the owner, he or she will understand the needs of the coffee and requisition the best equipment and supplies. And, as I have stated, the owner must be present on a daily basis in order to keep the program moving towards perfection. His or her passion will affect the staff greatly—keeping them excited as you all learn together. Passion, in my book, can be measured by how much work and effort one is willing to expend towards the stated goal. If the owner begins to be consumed with other aspects of the business—marketing, etc.—the espresso quality will deteriorate very rapidly. Staff morale quickly follows.

The beauty of an espresso business that makes a fine cup of coffee is that the customers are your best marketing tool. Word of mouth is king when it comes to the coffee business. People just love to brag up their favorite coffee place and bring in friends to try it out for themselves. Everything flows from the coffee.

In this way your ability to produce a great cup improves over time. The staff sees a true commitment to excellence in the passion of the macchinesti/owner who is willing to spend good money on equipment maintenance and quality ingredients.

Staff Culture

Staff culture evolves slowly in an organization. The interesting thing to me is that the people that make up your staff will, over time, intuitively hone in on your true priorities. Thus, if you indoctrinate people with a one-week training on espresso and service, but you're really more interested in short-term profit, the staff will pick up on this and begin to prioritize things differently in their work

habits. They will begin emphasizing speed over coffee quality, and the whole process will be reduced to simply "cranking out the product."

A top espresso barista is really an artist at heart. You, as an owner or trainer, must respect the beauty of a perfect cup, while at the same time guiding your staff performance around stated training goals. Show your respect by providing and maintaining the best possible equipment, and work with each individual's strengths and weaknesses. Over the years a culture of excellence forms among the staff as they gradually become the owners of their coffee skills, and trainers in the art.

XX
THE FUTURE OF CAFFE ESPRESSO
A MARKETING DISCUSSION

In Northern Italy, *caffe espresso* or *caffe expres* with steamed milk and sugar has been enjoyed for almost a century. It is useful—to get a hint what might be the enduring styles in the United States—to briefly examine the traditions surrounding the enjoyment of espresso.

In Northern Italy, *cappuccino* is steamed milk and espresso coffee served in about a 6- or 7-ounce cup. It is traditionally enjoyed in the morning with a roll called brioche—the typical Italian breakfast. Cappuccino can be ordered without foam, and often is. At the better bars, cappuccino does feature a heavy, velvet-like texture, but the defining characteristic is the volume of milk served with the coffee rather than the texture.

If you order a latte in Italy, the barman will pour you a glass of milk.

Espresso macchiato means espresso marked with a bit of milk and is usually enjoyed in the mid-morning, perhaps with a stirring of sugar.

For espresso without milk, two choices are common. One is called *espresso ristretto,* which means restricted coffee. In this option, the espresso pour is restricted to the most flavorful part of the shot and is the choice of most espresso connoisseurs when ordering. A single shot may be no more than 3/4 than of an ounce.

Espresso ristretto offers the greatest opportunity for the nuances of the coffee flavors to be present with a minimum of distracting caffeine. The natural caramelized sugars of a master roast will be maximized by this pour. A shot of coffee may be less than one ounce in this region when ordered ristretto.

The other option is *espresso lungo,* which means an espresso long pour with maybe a 1/2-ounce total volume. A lungo pour offers the most caffeine available from the coffee and a more alkaline cup than ristretto. Also, the texture may thin out a bit.

It is traditional to enjoy straight espresso with a stirring of white or turbinado sugar.

After dinner, many Italians enjoy *caffe corretto,* meaning espresso "corrected," with an infusion of a liqueur of some sort. This may take the function of the *digestivo,* a strong drink to aid in digestion of the meal. Exactly what is mixed with the espresso will vary by household and region.

Let me leave you with a prediction as to the fate of espresso coffee in the United States.

We are a health-conscious people, and soon we will reject the drinking of 12 to 16 ounces of milk per day with our tall latte. The adult body does not need this quantity of milk on a daily basis, not to mention those in our society who are lactose intolerant. Therefore, I believe that the culture will evolve into customers ordering less milk, such as cappuccino, which I've mentioned is about 6 to 7 ounces total.

With less milk, the flavor of the espresso becomes more apparent. With this in mind, espresso professionals who attend to the techniques, serve fresh coffee and keep their equipment clean will position themselves ahead of this evolving trend.

People will not want syrups or increasingly exotic concoctions if the coffee can be made to taste good on its own—made to taste as good as its aroma. Trends and fads will come and go, great coffee is eternal.

It has been said that if you learn to make a good cup of coffee the world will beat a path to your door. I can tell you from personal experience that this is true.

So 34 years later, the coffee has kept its promise to a very impressionable four-year-old boy. An aromatic promise of mysterious and imagined pleasures has been fulfilled in a little sweet-cream of a coffee, caffe espresso.

XXI
To Prepare Vivace Espresso

A one-sheet method to remove, laminate and place behind the espresso machine summarizing the proper techniques.

1. Pre-heat group head and porta-filter by running 2 ounces of water through the head with porta-filter in place. (Porta-filter should utilize double shot basket.)

2. Grind about 17 grams of coffee (two small chambers full in the doser).

3. Dry the coffee basket, then flap dosing lever on the grinder until all coffee is in the group basket. Be quick and precise.

4. Distribute evenly with edge of finger. Level of coffee before packing should be flush or just below the edges of the double group basket for most machines.

5. Pack levelly, tap once lightly to dislodge loose coffee, pack again with 30 pounds of pressure and a full twist on the packer as you release pressure to polish the coffee.

6. Just before putting porta-filter into the group head, let another 2 ounces of water through the head.

7. Insert group handle into group head. Extract a 1-1/2-ounce shot of espresso in 25-30 seconds. If it takes too long, make the grind a little coarser; if it comes out too quickly, make the grind a little finer. Serve immediately.

8. Remove group handle from head and release a 2-ounce sample to clear coffee oils out of the head.

9. Insert blind filter (it should be on a separate handle) and backflush the group.

Hourly Cleaning
Remove coffee basket from group and scrub with a Scotch Brite® pad.

Nightly Cleaning
1. Clean head by backflushing with espresso detergent.

2. Remove dispersal screen and porta-filter and soak them overnight in espresso detergent solution.

3. Scrub behind dispersal screen with Scotch Brite® pad.

4. Clean group gasket with Q-Tip® or green scrubber.

5. Remove and clean steamer tips with a pin or brush.

GLOSSARY

Barista	A bartender trained in espresso preparation.
Gaffe Latte	Espresso combined with steamed milk in a ratio of 6:1 (six parts or greater milk to one part espresso). Generally served in a 12-ounce cup.
Gaffe Espresso	Coffee made with pressurized brewing water wherein water pressure is between 8 and 9 bars of pressure, extraction time is between 18 and 30 seconds, total volume for a double shot is between 1 and 3 ounces, using 14 to 17 grams of freshly ground coffee with brewing water temperatures between 194 and 206 degrees Fahrenheit. *Also* carries the connotation that the coffee is prepared especially for an individual, upon request, to his or her preference.
Cappuccino	Espresso combined with steamed milk in a ratio of about 5:1 (five parts milk to one part espresso), served in a ceramic bowl-shaped cup of no more than 7-ounce volume.
Crema	A polyphasic colloidal foam created when pressurized brewing water brings soluble coffee flavors (mostly lipids) into solution during the brewing of an espresso shot.
Espresso Macchiato	Espresso combined with steamed milk in a ratio of about 1:1 (one part milk to one part espresso) with the milk added to the espresso to form a mark on the top of the espresso crema. (Literally, espresso marked with milk.)

Espresso a Lungo Espresso made by passing close to 3 ounces of brewing water through the ground coffee for a double shot. (Literally, espresso long.)

Espresso Ristretto Espresso made by passing close to 1-1/2 ounces of brewing water through the packed coffee for the double shot. (Literally, restricted espresso.)

Macchinesti The espresso (machine) specialist, trainer and quality assurance technician for a professional espresso program.

Porta-filter Portable coffee filter to be fitted with a single, double, or triple brewing basket in the preparation of espresso coffee.

Rosetta A flower pattern formed by pouring steamed milk into espresso coffee.

To order additional copies of:

ESPRESSO COFFEE
UPDATED PROFESSIONAL TECHNIQUES

Please send $27.95 plus $4.50 shipping and handling,
Washington residents please include 8.6% sales tax.

Make check or money order payable to:
Classic Day Publishing
2100 Westlake Avenue North, Suite 106
Seattle, Washington 98109
800-328-4348

If you prefer to use VISA or Mastercard (please circle appropriate card):

Card Number _____

Signature _____

Exp. date _____

_____ copies @ $27.95 ea.   _____

$4.50 Shipping & Handling   _____

Washington State residents add 8.6%   _____

Total enclosed   _____

Name _____

Address _____

City _____ State _____ Zip _____

Please list additional copies to be sent to other addresses on a separate sheet.